ALASKA CARIBOU
Ramblings & Ruminations

JAKE JACOBSON

Alaska's Favorite Real Life Wilderness Storyteller

PO Box 221974 Anchorage, Alaska 99522-1974
books@publicationconsultants.com—www.publicationconsultants.com

ISBN 978-1-63747-031-2

eBook ISBN Number: 978-1-63747-032-9

Library of Congress Catalog Card Number: 2021912416

Copyright 2021 Jake Jacobson

—First Edition—

All rights reserved, including the right of reproduction in any form, or by any mechanical or electronic means including photocopying or recording, or by any information storage or retrieval system, in whole or in part in any form, and in any case not without the written permission of the author.

J.P. "Jake" Jacobson
Alaska Master Guide #54
PO Box 1313
Kodiak, Alaska 99615
website: www.huntfish.us/
email: huntfish@ak.net

Cover photo thanks to my friend and frequent hunting guest, Bruce Moe.

Manufactured in the United States of America.

ALASKA CARIBOU: Ramblings & Ruminations
is the sixth book by Jake Jacobson on Alaskan topics.
His other books are:

ALASKA HUNTING: Earthworms to Elephants

ALASKA TALES: Laughs and Surprises

ALASKA FLYING: Surviving Incidents and Accidents

ALASKA BEARS: Stirred and Shaken

KODIAK ALASKA DEER: Stories, Sterility and Stewardship

Jake's books can be found at amazon.com and other good book stores or autographed copies can be ordered directly from Jake.

Contents

Introduction 7

Chapter One
Caribou Ramblings & Ruminations 11

Chapter Two
Ancient Hunters 19

Chapter Three
Caribou Attack 25

Chapter Four
Never Give Up 29

Chapter Five
1996 Guests From Florida 41

Chapter Six
A Pair Return to Trail Creek 49

Chapter Seven
2001 Muslims Strike 55

Chapter Eight
At Trail Creek, 2002 75

Chapter Nine
2003 Return of the Maneater 87

Chapter Ten
2004 A Great Season 101

Chapter Eleven
2005 Another Exceptional Year 125

Chapter Twelve
A Hoax and Reversal of Fortune 159

Chapter Thirteen
A Second Try for Caribou and Grizzly with Jake 165

Chapter Fourteen
Reno's Caribou 175

Chapter Fifteen
A Night on Heated Gravel 183

Chapter Sixteen
Franco and the Montanans 193

Chapter Seventeen
Women Who Hunt 213

Chapter Eighteen
The Guy Who Never Got His Deer 223

Chapter Nineteen
Clumsy Kills 227

Chapter Twenty
Spend an Extra Day 237

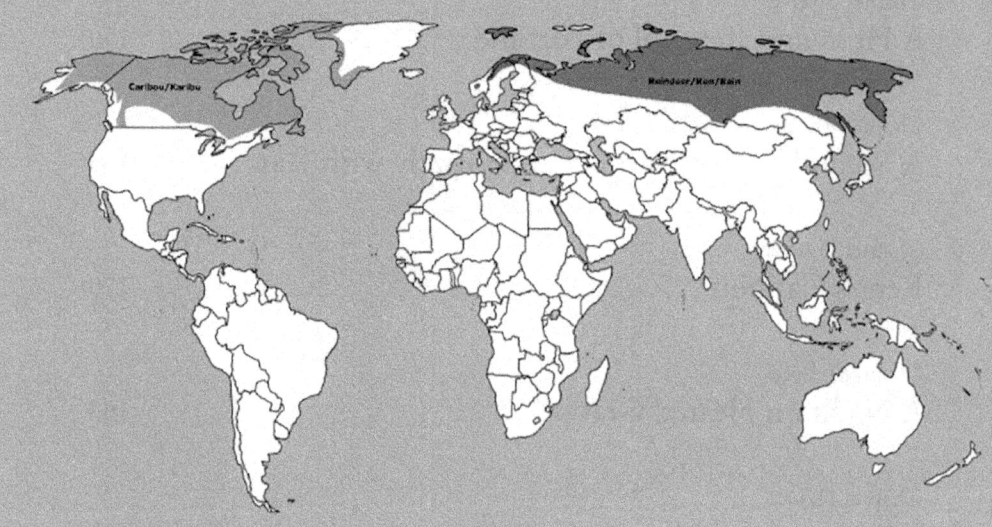

Distribution of caribou shown in the new world and reindeer in the old world.

Introduction

Rangifer tarandus is a northern hemisphere animal with no modern representation below the 50th parallel

For most hunters, the pursuit of wild game quarry has many rewards. First, there is the stimulation of the hunt. Preparation, anticipation and physically engaging in the pursuit of wild game has, since prehistoric times, been a healthy, stimulating activity for mankind. The uncertainty of outcome demands the hunter direct all his senses and skills to the present undertaking. The hunter must remain alert and focused if he is to be successful.

Rewards, in addition to personal satisfaction include the meat and other parts of the animal's body such as antlers, bones, hooves and skin for use in the manufacture of tools, clothes, or decoration of the hunter's home.

In many of the stories in this book I mention how the animal scored in the Alaska Professional Hunters' Association/Safari Club International Annual Big Three Competition. My primary motive for mentioning how the animal placed is to give the reader a means of judging the quality of the individual animal as compared with what is representative of its kind and what was taken throughout Alaska in that particular year.

Among modern trophy hunters many myths and misconceptions have arisen. When I arrived in Alaska in 1967 I was led to believe that all of the really large caribou and moose came from the Alaska Peninsula. But in 1984, the first year I entered guest trophies in the Big Three Competition, my guests took second and third place moose, and in 1985 a guest took the second place caribou - from northwest Arctic Alaska! By 2018 our guests had taken 65 First, Second, and Third place trophies for Caribou - 32, Moose - 7, Dall ram 7, Grizzly bear -7, Sitka Blacktail Deer - 7, Wolf -4 and Black Bear -1.

Many people believe that the really large members of each species were taken many years ago. The Alaska Big Three Annual Competition

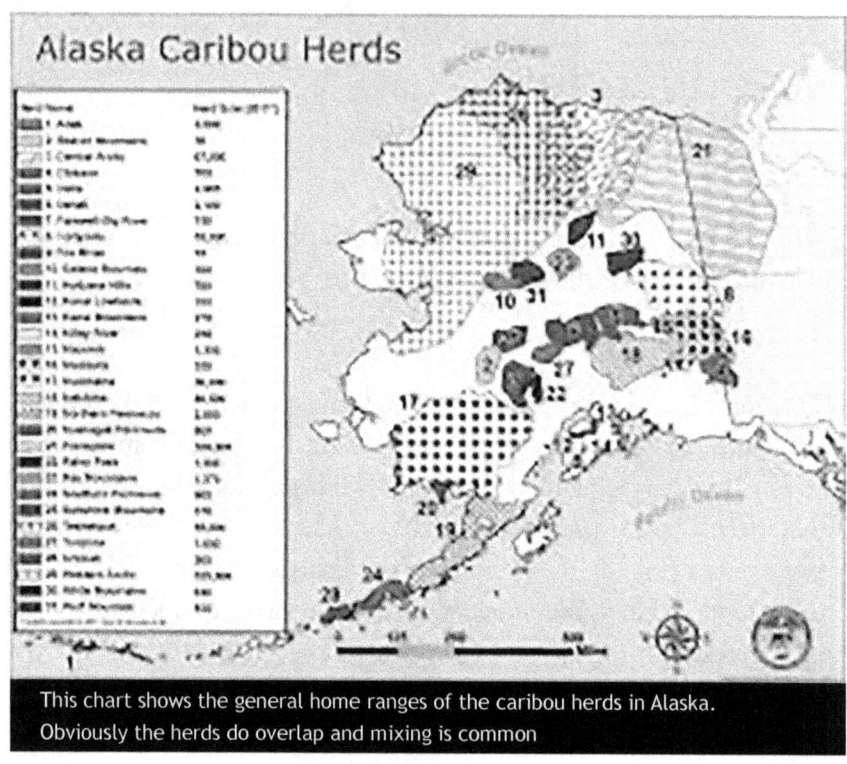

This chart shows the general home ranges of the caribou herds in Alaska. Obviously the herds do overlap and mixing is common

shows in which general area the largest animals of each year are taken and demonstrates that trophies are taken in modern times which are as large as those taken in the past. This is a partial confirmation of the success of game management.

Our guest hunters take great pleasure in receiving their plaque for first, second or third place animals. This makes another indelible memory from their hunt.

I was appointed to the Western Arctic Caribou Working Group in 2016.

Introduction

Western Arctic Caribou Herd
Satellite Collar History 1988-2004

The Western Arctic Caribou Herd has received a lot of attention since its precipitous drop in numbers in 1976. This map shows tracings of radio collared animals. Our lodge is located in one of the most heavily trafficked areas.

[9]

Chapter One
Caribou Ramblings & Ruminations

Caribou are the most successful big game animal in the Arctic. They are ruminants - even-toed ungulate mammals that chew the cud regurgitated from its rumen. The ruminants comprise cattle, sheep, antelope, deer, giraffes, and their relatives with a four-chambered stomach. Their digestive system is uniquely different from that of humans. Instead of one compartment to the stomach they have four. Of the four compartments the rumen occupies the largest section which is the main digestive center. Caribou mainly eat lichens in winter, especially reindeer moss. However, they also eat the leaves of willows and birches, as well as sedges, grasses and mushrooms.

In Alaska, caribou numbers exceed that of all other big game animals combined. With the same chromosomal data as the European and Asian reindeer, they are essentially the same animal, with some minor differences, such as the occasional "pinto" colored hides of reindeer, which are selectively bred for the more colorful hides, as the more noticeable hides are attractive to those who taylor skins. All "subspecies" can interbreed successfully.

Dozens of times I have read advertisements from guides and transporters in Alaska offering hunts for Mountain Caribou. The animals are found in mountains - and every other conceivable terrane, but the true sub species of Mountain Caribou exist primarily in British Columbia. Most caribou in Alaska are classified as Rangifer tarandus grantii, known commonly as Barren Ground Caribou.

There is an exception - one small herd of Woodland Caribou, the Chisana herd, is a non-migratory herd which resides between Alaska and Canada in the Wrangell-St. Elias area of Southcentral Alaska.

Trail Creek is named for the deeply rutted trails of tundra deer.

Annual fall migrations are somewhat haphazard, however the repeated use of routes is confirmed by the deeply rutted trails left by large herds of caribou.

Fall movements are triggered by the amount of daylight and weather rather than by an internal clock. Snow in the high country or a series of hard frosts will usually move the herd, as the days grow shorter.

A July post calving aggregation near the lodge.

In spring the cows are pregnant, and calving doesn't wait for the snow to melt. Calves are born from mid-May to early June. Calving areas are generally windblown and have good access to food sources

Of the recognized 32 herds of caribou in Alaska, the one that inhabits NW Arctic Alaska is called the Western Arctic Caribou Herd (WACH) and is the largest, with estimates of up to 490,000 animals during their recent population high.

For several years I was chartered to fly my super cub by the Alaska Department of Fish and Game on caribou surveys and other research projects, including documentation of wolf predation. The greatest amount of

Caribou on a snow drift, avoiding mosquitos.

Caribou standing in the breaking surf to escape insects.

time and effort spent in caribou management occurred during the spring calving season. Each of the herds has a distinct calving area and the WACH herd gathers for calving about 35 miles north of our lodge on Trail Creek. Cows begin to drop their calves during the first week of June and most are on the ground and running by June 10. Most cows two years of age or older produce a single calf every year. Twinning is extremely rare - I've never seen a set of twins in my more than fifty years of hunting and working with many thousands of caribou in Alaska.

Following calving, caribou split up into groups called "post calving aggregations" which roam through the mountains and west to the coast, sometimes traveling fifty miles or more in a single day. These movements are believed to be primarily insect driven. Often large groups of animals are seen standing in knee deep surf or gathered on snow drifts, as the cooler temperatures in those areas reduce mosquito and warble fly activity. Some animals remain throughout the summer in the high mountain meadows near our lodge, with the bulls just hanging around, making meat and growing antlers.

By fall, the calves, at age two and a half months, typically show small antlers. Caribou are the only deer species in which both males and females normally produce antlers.

Antler growth is completed by mid August. Between then and the first week of September most caribou shed their velvet. The initial blanched white appearance of the antlers is soon stained various shades of brown, depending on what vegetation is available for rubbing off the velvet and subsequent polishing of the antlers by rubbing them on branches and bushes.

In northwest Alaska, one can rely on the rut commencing on October 10, - almost to the day. Once the bulls enter the rut, I know of no other herbivore that carries such a pervasive and noxious stench. Having been advised of that early in my first year in the state, I never shot or allowed a guest to shoot a rutty bull. We quit hunting caribou bulls before October 10, and do not resume until after Thanksgiving.

Most of the older bulls shed their antlers between Halloween and Thanksgiving, Barren cows and a few of the younger bulls keep their headgear until April. Pregnant females normally retain their antlers until after the birth of their calf. A cow with one antler often indicates she carries no calf embryo - she is barren.

So with antlers at Christmas time, all of Santa's reindeer must have been female, including Rudolph!

In December, 1983 I was suffering the lonesomes worse than any other time in my life. My wonderful wife, Mae, had passed away in September and at first I just stayed home with my dog, Max, smoking cigars and drinking whiskey. Friends brought me meals, came to visit, and tried to cheer me up. I had a hard time even talking.

My buddy Hank came by one day and persuaded me to go with him on our snow machines to get some fresh caribou meat. I reluctantly agreed to do it. I'd been asked to be the town Santa Claus for various festivities

"Sport Hunter Gone Berserk" or "Poaching Hurts Us All"

and had been loaned a Santa suit. When we came in with some still unskinned caribou, I recognized this as an opportunity that should not be missed, so I made some photographs of Hank and my daughter, Sandy, showing an imaginary tragedy - the shooting of Santa. I used this one as a Christmas card and have since seen it on the internet.

Caribou are very gregarious animals and singles or small groups can often be lured to within rifle or bow range by the hunter merely hunching over with gun butt held high to be easily seen, as the hunter ambles along like a feeding caribou. Their curiosity rivals that of Pronghorns.

Caribou seem to be always on the move, browsing primarily on lichens, leaves of willows and other tundra plants such as mushrooms during the summer. By autumn they prefer dried sedges, blueberry stems, caribou moss and other lichens.

I've noticed that caribou show bloated abdomens more quickly after being killed than do other deer. That suggests to me that intense bacterial action is necessary to break down their coarse fodder.

Their sense of smell is well developed, but I believe they primarily depend on their eyesight to avoid predators, the primary one being wolves. Caribou usually do not tarry in brushy areas, preferring open country with good visibility. They seem to fly smoothly and effortlessly over the deep tussocks when alarmed.

Archaeological evidence indicates large fluctuations in caribou availability have been common in the past. Their population cycles are not well understood, but fortunately, from the late 1970s through the present, we in northwest Alaska have enjoyed an extended period of great abundance of these wonderful animals.

Some locations, like Onion Portage on the Kobuk River have been used by human hunters for millennia, as shown by caribou bone and antler artifacts in the rich prehistoric middens. Today, hundreds of local hunters converge on Onion Portage with firearms in early September. Yet in spite of heavy harvests for so long - practically forever - still the caribou continue to come by the same route.

The Trans Alaskan oil pipeline and location of bush villages seem to have little, if any, effect on caribou movements.

Our lodge is located on Trail Creek, so named for the great number of deeply rutted caribou trails that mark the valley. Most trails follow the general north/south drift of the valley, but many veer off to traverse the steep, barren mountains.

"No man knows the ways of the wind or the caribou" is an old Eskimo saying that sums up the nature and lack of predictability of these beasts as well as any explanation that I have heard.

I read that following the 1835 discovery of the rich whaling grounds in the NW Arctic, the use of firearms became common, the local caribou populations plummeted and native people were left without one of their main food sources.

Primarily due to the urging of missionary Sheldon Jackson, the federal government funded purchase of 1,250 reindeer from the Chukchi Siberian natives, which were transported across Bering Straits to the NW Alaska mainland by revenue cutters in the 1890s.

Herders from Lapland were brought in to instruct the local Inuits in reindeer husbandry. These semi-domesticated deer increased to over six hundred thousand by 1932. However, due to many of the deer wandering off with wild caribou and other factors, that number had dropped to twenty-five thousand by 1950.

My father in law, Chester Seveck, told me that he had personally shot dozens or sometimes hundreds of caribou at a time, as he tried to prevent his reindeer from running off with the migrating bands of wild caribou. That was accepted practice amongst old time reindeer herders.

When I first visited NW Alaska in 1967, the federal government maintained a Reindeer Service office in Kotzebue which employed a pilot and shotgunner for wolf control efforts as well as a secretary. That office was closed in 1974.

Later in the 1970s the Northwest Alaska Native Association (NANA) was given a reindeer herd and the company brought in some Icelandic horses and a helicopter to aid in managing the deer, but that operation also failed. Today one occasionally sees a few reindeer on Baldwin Peninsula south of Kotzebue.

There are some reindeer herds still being successfully managed on Seward Peninsula and points south.

Many Alaskans have told me that they did not care for the flavor of caribou meat, but I have always enjoyed it. In some cases I was able to give samples of meat from northwest Alaska to people who told me that they did not care for caribou, who later told me that the meat I had given them from the far northwest had a wonderful flavor, unlike any other caribou that they had eaten. I wonder if the large number of reindeer that were incorporated into the wild caribou of the region may partially explain the better tasting meat, or if it is due to the unique diet of the Arctic animals? I believe the more likely reason is the diet.

In April, 1968 I was working in Shungnak, on the Kobuk River when two men from the Atomic Energy Commission came through and tested everyone, including myself, for the presence of Cesium 137, a radioactive isotope produced by nuclear fission. This isotope was thought to have a half life of thirty years and was believed to have been generated by Soviet atmospheric nuclear testing and carried to the Alaskan tundra by the winds. They postulated that lichens absorbed the cesium, which was then incorporated into the caribou meat and finally deposited in the apex predators - humans and wolves. Their tests revealed cesium in local people to be many times higher than what was believed to be safe, but I never heard of any adverse consequences to people of the region.

However, I have always avoided eating caribou liver, as that organ acts as a filter and holds higher concentrations of cesium than other parts of the animal.

A caribou roast often shows a metallic color when sliced.

Caribou herds all seem to be subject to cycles of abundance and scarcity. The Western Arctic Herd fell from a quarter of a million animals in 1972 to about seventy-five thousand, or fewer, by 1976, due to a number of reasons, with wanton waste by local residents being the primary cause. Following that population's low point, annual recruitment was about thirteen percent until it reached four hundred and ninety thousand in 2003.

Caribou hooves, the left foot shows an injury.

Throughout this remarkable come back, there were an average of fifty bulls per one hundred cows.

Caribou make a clicking sound when they trot or run. Those unique sounds are attributed to tendons that snap over sesamoid bones in their feet. Some biologists think the clicking helps the members of a herd stay in contact, especially in snowstorms, foggy conditions, etc. The hooves of young calf caribou do not click.

Anything but elegant, caribou feet are well designed. When the hoof hits the ground it spreads into two large, concave cloves adding surface area which reduces the amount of sinking into snow, mud or other soft surfaces.

Those concave hooves also aid in digging through snow to reach buried lichens and other winter feed. In water the paddle-like shape of the hooves assist in swimming.

The name "Caribou" is thought to be derived from the Micmac Indian word "xalibu" which in that language means "pawer" or "shoveler."

Chapter Two
Ancient Hunters

Often in hunting, there comes a time to sit, observe and evaluate one's goals and situation - and to reflect on the here and now and what might have been last week or long before.

Years ago I was sitting on a hillside north of the lodge with my fine labrador, Zeke, sitting in contact with me. I wondered how long ago another man and his dog might have first done just that - in that same place. Artifacts left by prehistoric hunters in the area date back more than nine thousand years. Caribou have been coursing through the Trail Creek and adjacent valleys for exactly how long we do not know, but it is reasonable to assume that the presence or passage of caribou drew the ancient men here, just as caribou and other big game drew me to this location.

At my feet I saw one intact point, a couple broken points and several flakes of chert. It appeared that some ancient hunter had been here making projectile points as he waited for game.

We were primarily hunting caribou, so we chose a place that gave us a good view of an area that included the convergence of several side canyons and streams - just as the prehistoric hunters might have done. It seems that geographically and otherwise, some things don't change much over time.

Evidence from the Mesa site, approximately forty miles north by northeast of our lodge, dated by the accelerator mass spectrometry method, indicated that Paleoindians were hunting big game from that site some 9,700 to 11,700 years ago, but caribou were not abundant. Steppe bison were the primary prey of the Mesa people.

Historical records and prehistorical evidence suggest that frequent and dramatic population fluctuations have always occurred in Alaskan caribou herds. There was a 3,000 year absence of caribou in the Pleistocene or Ice

Zeke, my dog was as intent on seeing game as I was.

Age period which ended about ten thousand years ago.

During the early and mid-1970s most Alaskan herds declined. The statewide population declined from 415,000 in 1970 to 255,000 in 1977 (a decline of 39%). In contrast most herds increased from 1977 to 1989. The statewide population grew from 255,000 in 1977 to 729,000 in 1989.

Stone projectile points classified as Paleo-Indian points.

In 1972, as I was packing back to Trail Creek from a sheep hunt on the North Slope. About five and a half miles upstream from the cabin, my guest hunter and I stopped to rest at a stream bank where I noticed some fire-blackened and cracked rocks, indicating an old camp fire. I pocketed some chert flakes and later told the local Bureau of Land Management biologist about the site. Some years later a National Park Service archaeologist helicoptered to the site and took some samples. He found no evidence of caribou. His findings indicated the site was inhabited more than 9,000 years ago. It is reasonable to assume that the same or similar Paleoindians who used the Mesa site may have visited Trail Creek.

For prolonged periods of time in the ancient past, caribou have been mysteriously scarce, or absent. The mesa site artifacts indicate the

The mostly intact skull of a male *Bison priscus* which I found along the coast south of Kodiak, and about 170 miles south of Trail Creek lodge.

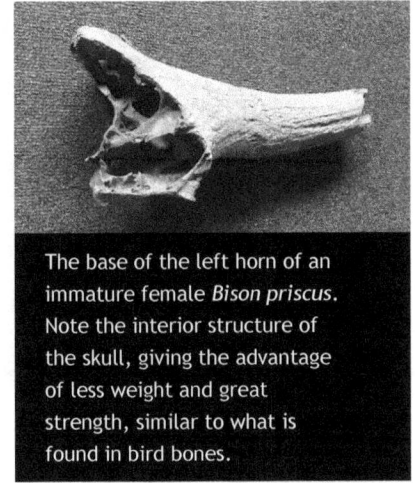

The base of the left horn of an immature female *Bison priscus*. Note the interior structure of the skull, giving the advantage of less weight and great strength, similar to what is found in bird bones.

Paleoindians subsisted primarily on Steppe Bison (*Bison priscus*) when caribou were not available. I assume a similar scenario existed on Trail Creek as I have found bits and pieces of prehistoric bison bones along the stream and cut banks.

As the arctic thaws, ancient permafrost recedes to reveal bits and pieces of ancient bison and, less commonly, muskoxen, but few traces of caribou from the distant past are found.

The Paleoindian cultures of temperate North America occupied that region between ca. 11,500 and 8500 years BP, and their primary subsistence resources were large Ice Age mammals. In arctic Alaska, the Mesa people were present during the same time period and subsisted on the same types of animals. Considering the identical technological and cultural elements, independent invention/cultural evolution, is unlikely and there can be no doubt that the Mesa Complex is part of the Paleoindian cultural tradition.

A succession of the Eskimo cultures began with the Denbigh Flint Complex people (ca. 4500 to 2500 years BP), who were followed by the Choris (ca. 2800 to 2200 years BP), Norton (ca. 2400 to 1800 years BP), and Ipiutak (ca. 1900 to 1200 years BP) cultures (Giddings 1964). The middens and artifacts from these cultures show varying degrees of caribou use.

Most recently caribou population change was demonstrated by a drastic crash in the arctic Alaska caribou population (Western Arctic Caribou

Herd), beginning ca. 1890 and continuing through the 1920s. As a result, between 1900 and 1930 the Brooks Range, and all but the coastal region of the North Slope, were abandoned by the native population. It was not until the early 1930s, as caribou numbers began to increase, that people began living in the interior region once again.

> **PLEISTOCENE.** A geologic time period beginning about 1.6 million years ago, and ending about 10,000 years ago, commonly referred to as the ice age.
>
> **PLEISTOCENE / HOLOCENE TRANSITION.** A period of several thousand years that spans the changing of the climate at the end of the ice age to conditions more like the present.

Pleistocene mammal species, bison, muskox, and caribou, were represented in the fossil record as present in the region between ca. 12,000 and 10,000 years BP.

There were basically two types of grazers inhabiting arctic Alaska during the late Pleistocene: ruminants, such as bison, muskox, and caribou, and monogastrics such as mammoth and horse.

Research indicates that caribou, which are by far the most numerous large mammal species through Holocene and recent times, appear to have been less abundant during the late Pleistocene, although they appear to be relatively common prior to and immediately following the last glacial maximum. Pleistocene (Ice Age) caribou accounted for only about 3% of the regional biomass, whereas in recent times, their regional biomass level has been around 90%.

Caribou numbers were not high enough for them to be a reliable subsistence resource much before 7500 years BP (Before Present). It is worth noting that at the same time, caribou numbers appear to be so low that they are absent from the fossil record, and probably were not a commonly used subsistence resource.

The prehistoric peoples of northwest Alaska were primarily meat eaters. Native Brooks Range people's diet consisted of no more than 3% plant material.

I am sitting on a unique prehistoric village site on the shore of a large Brooks Range lake that has a reliable amount of fish and big game animals sufficient to feed several dozen people and was likely used throughout the year.

As caribou numbers increased and spread over the landscape, human hunters similarly increased and spread. Ancient people departed the coast areas for new haunts in the interior. New villages appeared in places that supported sufficient animals to feed the people. When the availability of sufficient food declined, the villages shrank or were abandoned.

Caribou flesh and parts were consumed in a variety of ways: boiled, roasted, raw, frozen or dried, with boiling and roasting the most common. To boil the flesh, hot stones were often added to a water-filled wood vessel, caribou stomach, or pit lined with caribou skin. Netsilik Inuit and Chukchi frequently ate raw meat and sometimes dipped it into seal oil before consumption. Inuit ate mostly raw meat, preferring it slightly fermented, but occasionally roasted or boiled as well. Communities would sometimes have a feast on the raw meat of a freshly killed caribou. The animal would be brought to the centre of the lodge and guests would sit on the floor around it. The host would skin the carcass and the hide would be spread on the floor to act as a dish or reservoir for the blood. The guests, all armed with knives, would help themselves to the meat until only skin and skeleton remained. The blood, a delicacy, was scooped with horn spoons or skin cups and consumed with the flesh. So I have been told by elders.

Chapter Three

Caribou Attack

After traveling throughout Alaska for two years and spending a lot of time in villages of the northwest region as an itinerant Indian Health Service dentist, I decided to settle in Kotzebue. The population was about 1,600 people with a higher number of sled dogs. The number of private automobiles could probably be counted on one's fingers and toes. A full time government dentist was stationed in Kotzebue, but I figured I could make a living by flying to rural communities that had no dentist, especially if I acquired an aircraft and developed sufficient skills in negotiating the weather, terrane and minimally maintained airports of rural Alaska - and maintaining my machine where certified mechanics were in short supply..

In my travels I saw other enterprises that piqued my interest, such as commercial bush flying, gold mining, and most interesting of all, guiding hunters and fishermen.

Rural people received me graciously and often invited me to join them in their activities. I preferred to travel by dog sled rather than the increasingly popular snow machines, but tending dogs would make too many demands on my time. I had to get a snow machine.

As has always been my way, my means of transportation need only be functional, sportiness did not appeal to me. The most popular brands of "Sno-go" at the time were Arctic Cat, Evinrude, Polaris and Ski-Doo. The least expensive was the one cylinder SnoJet. I purchased a SnoJet from Hanson Trading Company in Kotzebue for six hundred dollars in 1969 - brand new! Most of my use would be in or near town as I'd had some bad experiences with sno-gos and was leery of the infernal machines, anyway.

Of course my buddies, riding the more popular and expensive brands referred to my machine as a "SnoShit." But it got me by.

In December, 1970 caribou were coming right through the streets of Kotzebue. Some cab drivers carried a rifle and would pause in transporting a passenger to shoot a caribou, then retrieve it to take home or give to the passenger.

I was invited to go up the Noatak River on a caribou hunt with some local men. It was not difficult to approach the animals, make a clean neck or head shot and load them into a hardwood basket sled to haul home.

I recall eating some agootuk on that trip, a local treat consisting of caribou fat whipped to a froth with seal oil and caribou meat or fish. One batch I was offered had some fruit cake sweets in it as well. It was mighty tasty in that twenty below weather. That memory has stuck with me over more than five decades.

The animals were focused on moving south and away from the deep snow and fierce cold in the far north. Our strategy was to find a herd of caribou, anticipate their trajectory, set up in whatever cover might be available and select the animals we wanted when they came within range. In open areas, too many of the hunters would drive their fast machines right up to the caribou and shoot the panicked animals. I was offended by that and did not participate in such methods.

Once I had my sled loaded with four caribou carcasses, I had enough. But some of my companions kept shooting until the caribou were gone or the hunter ran out of ammunition.

With my heavily laden sled and rifle in its scabbard I began the slow trip back to town. But two very young hunters in our group wanted more meat - or just more killing. One of the fellows had run out of bullets, so he tried to run down an immature bull. The animal turned and tried to fend off its pursuer. When the man on the machine gave up, the young bull persisted in trying to impale the human, until the snow machiner turned and sped away. I was happy to see the combative caribou run off to join his large herd.

My sympathies were with the lone caribou. I felt any animal so treated was being abused. But this valiant little bull refused to be knocked down and eventually escaped.

Caribou Attack

My first snow machine. New cost was $600

One young bull refused to be run down.

One scene of heavy harvest .... or slaughter. A large kill like this would require more than one trip back to town loaded with meat.

Jake with Penthouse Pet of November, 1977, Debra Zullo

Chapter Four
Never Give Up

Its preferable of course, to have all the sought after trophies secured well prior to the last scheduled day of the hunt, but Murphy rides with us all, it seems. And last minute trophies can be so very sweet! Many animals are taken in the last hours or minutes of a hunt.

Over the past fifty-four years of hunting and guiding in Alaska I recall many situations that culminated in eleventh hour success. Here are a few of them.

At a show in Corona, California, put on by Dick Haldeman (brother of Nixon's man, Bob Haldeman, I spent some unique spring days. Thanks to my friend Criag Boddington, I was listed on the program as a guest speaker from Alaska, which gave me a huge boost with making bookings! I booked a pair of attorneys and a fellow who worked for the City of Los Angeles as a preditor/nuisance animal controller. Due to so many participants in the show an Arizona guide and I were asked to share a booth with Penthouse magazine. Those lovely Penthouse models drew a lot of prospective hunters to our booth. Some of those who stopped by were actually interested in hunting big game in Alaska, but, for sure, the ladies baited in many "hunters" who hardly glanced at our photographs - they just scrutinized the girls. Some asked if one or more of the models worked for me and might be at the lodge during the hunting season. It pained me to tell them that none of those ladies were scheduled to accompany us on the hunts. That disappointed some of the prospective "hunters"!

Among other hunters I booked the two attorneys from Los Angeles, Tom and Steve. Steve brought his twelve year old son, Zack.

Our friend Tom collected his grizzly, a surprise wolf while fishing, and some small game, but caribou had eluded him in spite of our best efforts to give him an opportunity to harvest a tundra deer.

Tom's presence at the lodge and in the field was an ongoing delight. This professional advocate was forever optimistic and confident that he would prevail over the weather and other difficulties we seemed to be facing daily.

Tom was perhaps the most well read guest we had hosted at the lodge on Trail Creek. And his memory was remarkable. He was forever coming up with appropriate, impressive quotes from recognized greats of literature as well as unknown wits. I suspect that many of his uncredited quotes were of his own creation.

Toward the end of his booking period, Tom found his grizzly, not in the riparian brush or berry patches where we encounter most of the grizzlies, but high in the mountains.

When he examined his freshly killed bear he spontaneously burst forth with a quote from William Shakespeare:

"And gentlemen in England now a-bed
Shall think themselves accurs'd they were not here,
And hold their manhoods cheap whiles any speaks
That fought with us upon Saint Crispin's day."

Evening libations seemed to bring out many entertaining quotations from Tom. On hunting pursuits he told us, "If God didn't want men to hunt, He wouldn't have given us plaid shirts."- so Johnny Carson said.

"Deep in the guts of most men is buried the involuntary response to the hunter's horn, a prickle of the nape hairs, an acceleration of the pulse, an atavistic memory of his fathers, who killed first with stone, and then with club, and then with spear, and then with bow, and then with gun, and finally with formulae." So claimed Robert C. Ruark, in Horn of the Hunter.

Tom was one of three guests at the lodge for that booking and only he and young Zack had not filled all their tags. Zack at age twelve, was content to stay near the lodge in hope of a big bull wandering near, as commonly happens, but Tom wanted to get out and stretch his endurance. Pushing his limits was almost as attractive to him as collecting a caribou.

The morning before the final day we awoke to a quarter mile visibility in snow. There was little wind, so the compromised range of vision lingered until nearly noon. Tom was chomping at the bit to head north from whence he imagined fresh caribou would be coming. My assistant guide Ted was eager to get out of the building too, so the pair struck off up the creek.

Young Zack and his Dad, Steve, remained at the table content to play cribbage and glass from the windows. I sawed up some dead wood in preparation for an evening sauna, and so passed the day.

I filleted a salmon and got macaroni and cheese ready, tossed a salad and got the fixin's for fresh baked brownies to go in the oven after the saunas.

The snow was vanishing at ground level but persisted at levels a few hundred feet from the valley floor. The temperature hovered right around freezing which caused small rocks to stick to the bottom one's boots, making the already slick conditions that much more stumble-prone.

About 4pm I fired the sauna and placed four old square sided gas cans full of water atop the barrel stove to heat. That makes a wonderful, refreshing bath after an extended sweat in the sauna room.

Steve, Zack and I took our sauna, then I washed out some of my socks and undies. Wanting everyone to have a hot supper I held off on putting the salmon in the oven until, finally, just at dark, I saw Ted and Tom coming.

They had a fine story for us.

Just past Break Ankle canyon they came upon a medium sized grizzly which was intent on digging out voles, in between munching on berries. They passed within a hundred yards of the preoccupied bruin, which was never aware of their presence. That would have been a much easier kill than the one Tom had made a few days earlier. Murphy smiled, I'm sure.

The men walked to the "bear stairs" on Current Creek where they sat for an hour, eating their lunch and glassing for caribou, but they found none.

Tom wanted to go further north, so he and Ted slipped and stumbled their way to the next side drainage, which we call Summer Canyon. They spotted a lone bull caribou about a mile back into the steep canyon. It appeared to be a very good trophy, so miserable conditions or not, they proceeded to stalk the big bull.

There was no cover to conceal their advance, but the bull was busy stuffing its belly, allowing the men to approach to within three hundred yards. Ted told Tom that if the animal spooked it was only a few strides from the crest of the mountain and could be out of sight in seconds.

Success! Ted quickly made a photo and began to butcher the animal.

Tom elected to shoot and he shot well. His 30:06 projectile caught the bull just behind the withers, breaking its back and putting it down. It slid a few yards in the snow before coming to a full stop.

Tom said "Let us pray it toboggans its way to the bottom of the hill, lest we have to surmount these slippery stones to reach that fine beast." But that was not to be. The dead caribou hung up only a few meters below the place it was shot. The men spent more than half an hour getting to the carcass.

The bull had double shovels, decent overall dimensions and was well balanced, making it a fine trophy.

Tom spewed forth with number of entertaining quotes, among which were: "Hunts are rather like snowflakes and women. No two are quite alike." which he attributed to my friend and frequent booth partner at SafariClub Shows, Peter Hathaway Capstick,

Ted had the meat on his packboard and the antlers and cape secured to the board Tom used and they began the three and a half mile return to the lodge.

Zack appears to be incredulous at his last minute trophy.

The skies cleared but the overcast meant early darkness. The two men proceeded as rapidly as prudence and the risk of injury permitted. They experienced only minor mishaps, none of which lamed either man.

I directed them to the sauna, telling them to watch the time as I would put the fish and brownies in the oven in precisely thirty minutes.

Only young Zack had an unfilled tag.

Snow had melted from the runway, so the next morning I flew Tom to Kotzebue with his gear, caribou rack and meat. I dropped him at my sod shack in town, refueled and landed at the lodge in a bit over three hours.

I saw Ted coming from across the river with a load of meat. Shortly after I departed Ted spotted a lone bull on the cut back west of the lodge.

He took Zack and Steve and in a few minutes Zack knocked the bull down. His tag was filled! This bull had a wonderful left shovel and its antlers were bloody, having shed the velvet in the last twenty-four hours. It was a young animal, but it filled the bill for us all.

I made a quick flight back to town and returned for Steve. All was arranged for the trio to depart on Alaska Airlines on the morning flight.

The first surprise last minute caribou.

During the spring of 1974 I convinced myself that we should have a small cabin at the homestead site. Grizzly bears were always present and people staying in our wall tent were nervous about the big beasts. Any cabin beats a tent. So I made a graph paper blueprint, then split full sheets of plywood lengthwise to permit loading into a Cessna or Beaver. I tacked together the twelve foot by twelve foot cabin in our yard and numbered the pieces for ease of assembly at the site.

In April, 1974 I used the local Civil Air Patrol Beaver on hydraulic wheel skis to haul in the pre-cut lumber and siding for a small cabin. The bog adjacent to the homestead site was frozen and the snow was blown smooth, making a wonderful landing strip of over two thousand feet in length. I taxied close to the site for the cabin where I off loaded the materials on some large hummocks in the bog. I covered the pile with canvass tarps and crisscrossed the pile with ropes and old fishing net to keep it from blowing away in the big winds that often visit the valley.

By early July snow had melted from the area and I took my wife Mae, our daughter, Sandy, and my sister Pat to the site in my Cessna 180. I went back to town for tools, a wood stove, nails, rolled roofing, etc. and took that load to the site in the Super Cub.

I returned in about three hours and found the ladies had packed all the materials to the building site, so we got to work.

We had the small shelter assembled with a roof and door in place by the end of the day. Pre cut lumber and plywood made it easy.

In a light drizzle the next day I nailed the rolled roofing in place, installed two windows, hooked up the wood stove and build some "furniture" including two beds, a table and used aircraft gasoline boxes for shelving. This was so much better than our wall tent!

We had figured on three days for the project, so we had a full day to go fishing and maybe find fresh caribou meat.

The next morning as we were carrying things to the cub, a lone bull caribou came wandering up the runway. We awarded it with a free trip to Kotzebue.

Sandra, Mae and Pat with our fresh meat.

Later that summer we all went up to do more work on the little cabin and enjoy the place. This time, the day before our departure, we were blessed with a lone bull caribou that the ladies harvested and we took to town.

After the large post calving aggregation movement up the valley in July, many single or small groups of bulls remained in the valley, just making meat and growing antlers.

Mae, Pat and Sandy with a meat bull.

Many similar handy harvesting incidents would take place at or near the cabin over the next fifty years.

In August and September, 1972, my first booked hunting guest came from Montana and brought his teen aged son. We encountered many Dall sheep and frequently observed grizzly bears, but the hunters had only purchased tags for caribou. We were near the end of the booking period and it looked like we were about to be skunked. Then, after I had loaded the Cessna 180 and was ready to start the engine, a fine bull emerged from West Bowl and my dog, Zeke and I took the fellow across the river to make a stalk. Lone animals are much easier to approach than a band of many eyes and noses. At a hundred and fifty yards the fellow made a nice shot and he had his bull.

In 1998 I booked a German manufacturer and his friend. They had a unique story and relationship. During World War II he German's father had

It seemed that Zeke was at least as pleased as the hunter and I were.

military contracts with the government and could select men and boys from the concentration camps to serve in his factory. The man met a young jewish boy from France and was immediately impressed with the youth. He selected him for service and the grateful Frenchman performed exceedingly well. After the war, the manufacturer kept the young Frenchman on his staff. The young man was still serving the son of the industrialist when the German booked to hunt with me. He brought the Frenchman with him and bought him a caribou tag.

But it was late September and most of the caribou had long since headed south. It looked as if the Frenchman would have no opportunity to take an animal.

I had taken the German to town in hope that before it came time to fly the Frenchman, he might luck out with a caribou. I returned about midday and there had been no action, so I loaded the fellow's gear and as he was about to climb into the Super Cub, a lone bull appeared from nowhere and decided to visit the runway. Quickly the Frenchman dug out his ammunition, loaded his rifle and took the big bull.

My assistant guide Ted, with the Frenchman's dandy bull.

Note the orange cone marking the threshold of the runway. Once again we were blessed with an end of the hunt animal.

In 1994 I had taken my son, Martin, and grandson Spencer, to the lodge for some berry picking, steam fishing and perhaps ptarmigan and caribou hunting. On our day of departure I was changing the oil in the cub when Martin and Spencer came walking from down creek with some freshly caught Arctic Char and a couple of Willow ptarmigan. They reported they had seen no caribou. However I saw a lone bull following them up the runway. Caribou are gregarious creatures and often lone caribou will come close to people if they have not smelled them.

After hearing of them not seeing any caribou I suggested they turn around. They were amazed to see the mature bull about a hundred yards away and still coming. Resting his Dad's rifle on the horizontal stabilizer of the aircraft, Spencer dropped the animal within sixty yards of the plane.

It was another sweet gift and at age eight years, this was Spencer's first big game animal harvest.

Back not too long ago guest hunters, both American and foreign could harvest up to five caribou per year, while local subsistence qualified users could take fifteen animals per day - year 'round!

Often a guest hunter would shoot a respectable bull, then have an opportunity to take a more impressive trophy. Sometimes it happened that the hunter took a superb bull, only to find an even more impressive trophy. It was good to be able to continue to hunt. The meat was never wasted. What we did not use in camp filled our freezer for winter use, was given to family members and distributed to local folks in Kotzebue.

This bull had plenty of long top points, a double shovel and scored over

On this guest's first day in the field he took this fine animal.

four handed points. Our guest was ecstatic. He was a deer hunter from Illinois. The headgear of this caribou clearly blew away his finest deer rack.

The lucky hunter with his second magnificent caribou.

We went on with hunting a Dall ram and grizzly bear, but on his final day at the lodge, my friend Ted spotted a bull with a high scoring rack and the hunter tagged his second magnificent caribou a mile north of the lodge. We all felt lucky and I predicted that both of his animals might well place in the top three in the annual Big Three Competition.

The hunter elected to ship his two sets of antlers home, packaged together, as excess baggage. I suggested that he ship it via insured air freight, but he decided otherwise.

The airline company would only ship the package as far as Anchorage where he would have to claim the container, then take it to another airline for shipment to Illinois. When he arrived at the baggage claim console he could not find his large package. He immediately told the baggage attendant that he was missing an unmistakably large piece, but it was not found. The attendant told the hunter that just prior to his arrival at the claim area, a large package had been carried out by someone. That must have been his piece with the two large caribou racks. Those exceptional racks were never recovered for the man.

This guest of mine had exceptional good fortune in being able to collect two outstanding animals. He was keen to take the trophies with him to avoid time delays and possible damage or loss, only to find both the trophies had been stolen from the baggage claim in Anchorage. It is good that he had the photographs.

I made copies of photos and posted with several taxidermists in Anchorage but no one reported seeing either rack.

"The best laid plans of mice and men often go awry."

Chapter Five
1996 Guests From Florida

In 1996 we greeted a delightful group of three friends from Florida. All were involved in agriculture. Rex was a land owner and farmer, Henry was an entomologist while Tom farmed and ran a pest control business. From the moment Tom's feet hit the tarmac at the Kotzebue airport, it was all fun and laughter with this fellow. Tom had a lot of good jokes and he knew how to tell them.

This group had made several trips to Montana in pursuit of elk and deer. This was the first time to Alaska for each man.

The Western Arctic Caribou Herd (WACH) was near its peak of approximately half a million animals - double its estimated population of 242,000 in 1972 and a remarkable increase over its lowest number in 1976 which was estimated to be only fifty to seventy-five thousand animals.

Caribou herds have long been known to fluctuate wildly, but the recruitment of this herd was extraordinary. Unlike most types of deer, caribou do not drop twin calves, so the remarkable sustained increase in numbers was thought to be due to near ideal range and weather conditions with no unusual predation or disease influences. Accordingly, the Alaska Department of Fish and Game set the annual bag limits at 5 animals of either sex for non-residents. The daily limit for Alaskan residents was **5 caribou per day** and for local rural residents the limit was a most generous **15 caribou per day!**

Grizzly bears were increasing in number, but a lottery drawing was required to hunt a bear. Only Tom had been drawn for a Grizzly permit.

Upon arrival the the lodge on Trail Creek the three men marveled at how comfortable the accommodations were. After seeing my sod shack in Kotzebue and the rest of the little town, they were mentally prepared for far less. Bands of caribou dotted the hills on both sides of the valley.

We had ample time the first afternoon to sight in the rifles. Our guests were surprised to see the caribou were not disturbed by the shooting. In the steep mountains the sounds of tumbling rocks are common, which seems to condition the animals to such noises. Deer or elk would not be so indifferent to the sound of multiple rifle shots.

We filled out the paperwork and, at their request, I sold each man two caribou metal locking tags. It looked pretty certain that they would have plenty of opportunities to take at least two bulls each.

As we enjoyed a final cup of coffee after breakfast, Henry spotted a medium bull standing on a cut back just off the end of the runway. Tom and Rex agreed that Henry could be the one to take the first animal as he had not scored on a recent elk hunt. I mentioned that we would likely get chances at larger bulls, but Henry wanted to take this one.

I urged each man to try to shoot their animals in the neck, as the meat is so tasty, we wanted to lose as little as possible. As guests they were entitled to take half of the usable meat home, but few hunters actually took much, if any, meat. Meat in excess of our needs would be distributed to family and friends in Kotzebue.

We took our time moving through the willows toward the cut bank. Henry was nervous, but when time came to shoot, he did his job well. The bull immediately hit the ground and rolled down the slope with a broken neck.

This animal and a dozen others were within the boundaries of my deeded eight acres, so we spilled the guts in plain sight of the lodge windows, skinned the critter and used the three wheeler and trailer to take it to the meat rack. It doesn't get much easier than that.

Within an hour a "conspiracy" of ravens was squawking and hassling each other at the gut pile. Good news! This would not affect caribou, but it might well bring in wolves, a bear, or even a wolverine.

Small bands of caribou were lazily ambling down the valley from the north, eventually coalescing into larger herds as they headed south. As usual, the first of the migrating caribou groups were composed of cows, calves and a few younger bulls. The big bulls typically join the crowd as the days shorten and the temperatures drop. The first blowing snow storm on the north slope usually hastens the southward movement of the tundra deer.

1996 Guests From Florida

The next day we all sat on the ancient glacier moguls east of the lodge, transfixed on the hundreds of caribou meandering about the valley as they gradually moved downstream on their several hundred mile journey to their winter grounds.

In my letter to guests I mention the need for hip boots, calf length rubber boots, slippers for the lodge and thongs for the sauna.

A week before departing Florida, the three friends met to discuss the trip, what to bring, and so forth. As they went through my list of necessities, Henry indignantly announced that he "wasn't going to wear no danged thong."

Tom and Rex instantly recognized that they had an opportunity for a good hoo-raw on Henry. Neither explained to Henry that by thong, I meant what some call flip-flops - for the feet.

Tom began a long blathering extemporaneous explanation about how Arctic Eskimo custom was for men to never appear completely naked, even in the presence of other men, otherwise a hunter risks the wrath of the Gods and bad luck in hunting. In old times whole villages had starved due to indiscretions involving naked adult men. Henry did not question this unlikely story. But coming from Tom, he should have known better.

So Tom asked his wife to sew together a frilly-dilly thong for presentation to Henry when the time was right.

One afternoon it seemed a good idea to take a sauna as human body odors were becoming noticeable to everyone. Tom could not locate the fancy, ultra feminine g-string for Henry, but his wife had placed a plain black one in his bag. It would have to do.

Henry wearing his thong.

Rex, ever modest, entered the sauna first and seated himself on the top bench with a towel around his midsection. Tom and Henry peeled out of their hunting clothes in the outer section of the sauna building. Tom delayed his final disrobing as he waited for Henry to pull on the thong. Once Henry had his crotch cloth in place, Tom reminded him that we needed a bucket of tempering water from the creek. Henry dutifully proceeded to perform that chore.

[43]

I was in place with my camera when Henry returned from fetching the creek water and snapped a photograph as Tom and Rex roared in laughter. Then we explained to Henry the various meanings of the word "thong."

Henry promised appropriate retribution, but I am not aware of what his revenge might have been or when it was effected.

The caribou kept coming down the valley, but large numbers of mature bulls had not showed up after a full week of steady traffic. Antler development varies from year to year with some years offering exceptional development and others poor choices of trophies. After decades of wondering, I have so far not been able to predict the degree of antler development in advance. I suspect the amount of fly and other insect activity may be a major factor. Antler development may be influenced by temperature, the amount of rainfall, or who knows what other imponderable considerations. This was beginning to look like a poor year for antler development in both caribou and moose in my area.

We struck off early one morning to a favorite observation point that we call the South Overlook. From that point, about one thousand feet above the valley floor, we could see Trail Creek valley as it broadens and is joined by Popple Creek about five miles south of the lodge.

Before we had reached the South Overlook I noticed a small band of caribou running hard to the north. This was counter to the prevailing movement of the herds. Sure enough, right behind the fleeing caribou came two adult grey wolves in hot pursuit.

I alerted my guests to the wolves, told them to keep quiet and put a bullet up the spout. Then I let out a practiced howl.

The running wolves stopped and looked our way. After a few seconds I let out another howl. The two lobos ceased their pursuit and came on a dead run in our direction. Were they coming to assist a pack mate, or to attack a stranger. Who could know?

We could easily follow the wolves as they came toward us, but we would lose sight of them when they approached the base of the slope we occupied. I told the three hunters that I expected the wolves to pop up over the edge of the hill we were on. The range would be less than one hundred yards. Upon gaining that elevation I figured the wolves would stop to look and listen. I told the hunters to not hesitate to shoot as soon as they had a decent opportunity and to keep shooting until both wolves were lying still on the ground or were out of range. I advised the hunters to hunker down near a hummock and get comfortable for shooting.

After about three minutes the scenario I predicted happened just that way.

Henry was in the midst of a bowel evacuation when the wolves appeared, but he hastily brought up his trousers and grabbed his rifle. He didn't get his pants fully up and buckled until the shooting was over, for which we all give him a sound ribbing.

The larger wolf, a male I assume, paused briefly then came on a trot in our direction. Tom fired and the wolf went down, hit in the chest. Rex and Henry were shooting at the other wolf, which had turned and was going full speed toward the edge of the hill. It would soon be out of sight. Tom began trying to hit the second animal. Wolves are always quick to depart at the sound the first shot.

Tom's wolf struggled to stand up, then began to move back to the edge fo the hill. It was wobbly, but seemed to be gaining steadiness and speed with every step.

I hollered at Tom to shoot his wolf again, but he was reloading and the big lobo made his way over the edge.

A fair amount of discussion among the three Floridians took place over why so many shots had been missed, and such. I told everyone to load their magazines, but leave no live rounds in the chamber as we took up the pursuit. Given how hard Tom's wolf went down initially, I fully expected to find it lying dead within a hundred yards or so.

In a few minutes we were at the edge of the hill and I found several large splotches of dark red blood. It looked like arterial blood. Tom's wolf was bound to have bled out already, or so I figured. With a little fresh snow on the ground, the trail was easy to follow. We stayed with the wounded wolf's route for over two hours and covered about a mile and a half. The blood was decreasing and the animal had run straight up a very steep bank, which is not indicative of a badly wounded animal.

We did not find the wolf. This was the second wounding loss for me and first wounded animal I, or my guests had lost since 1984 when I could not locate a badly wounded Grizzly until it had spoiled and was being scavenged by ravens.

I feel terrible about wounding and losing any animal, even a rabbit!

As usual, we ascended the eastern side hill for the return trip. From midway up the side of the valley we had the best visual advantage possible, but we saw only cow caribou with calves.

Hoping to see ravens on the carcass of the wounded wolf, the next day we went south again. Just after crossing East Bowl Creek I spotted a Grizzly about two miles away browsing in a berry patch across Trail Creek and near the shale cliffs of Thunder Ridge. We all hustled toward the bruin, losing sight of it for brief periods as we, and the bear, traveled. It took a little over half and hour to reach the slope the bear was using, however it was another forty minutes before the busily feeding animal presented Tom with a reasonable shooting opportunity. With a good rest, at about one hundred and twenty yards Tom's bullet smacked the bear just behind the right shoulder. I thought it was a good hit.

That bear exploded straight up in the air about three feet, then came down the slope toward us. Henry asked if they all should shoot. I said, "No, it's Tom's bear." Tom in the excitement missed two shots which struck rocks just in from of the bear. At the second shot, the bear turned hard right and headed downhill toward a dense clump of willows. Tom hit the bear two more times as it tried to escape. After the last shot the bear seemed to deflate just before it collapsed in its tracks.

Tom and his mountain Grizzly

Everyone was puffing petty hard from the excitement. Henry was sure that we had been charged. However I believe the bear was highly excited and had no idea where we were. That was typical bear behavior, but easily misinterpreted, especially if the beast is hurtling your way.

This boar grizzly was well furred and rolling in fat. I packed the two hams to the cabin. Like pork, bear meat should be thoroughly cooked, but it is always tender and flavorable, if their diet is primarily berries, as is the case for bears on Trail Creek. The fat makes a tasty gravy to go with the meat and potatoes.

We were back at the lodge before mid-afternoon, so I positioned the hunters on the east moguls to glass for big caribou as I fleshed and salted the bear hide.

The next morning we headed up the creek. Caribou were still coming and little bands of the tundra deer pock- marked the terrane everywhere we looked.

As often happens, ravens were in attendance at this sustained migration. I counted twenty-two of the intelligent black scavengers from the lodge windows. Normally, along with ravens, one can expect to find wolves, so we kept our eyes and ears on full alert.

We sat and glassed for an hour at the North Overlook before moving further northwest. About six and a half miles from the lodge we found a large band of mature bulls. The terrane made moving in for a close shot easy and when all were settled on a good bull, the shooting began. Both Tom and Rex dumped their first targets, then, out of the milling confusion of caribou, each shot one more. Henry had planned to take only one animal but he wounded his and in his haste to dispatch it, he shot a second bull. So we had six caribou to carry more than six miles home.

Tom's bull scored best of the bunch and placed number three in the APHA/SCI annual Big Three statewide competition.

Henry, Tom and Rex with Tom's bull.

Tom, Henry and Rex with Henry's palmated bull.

Rex and his bull from way up the valley.

There was plenty of daylight left so we cut the animals up for packing. I carried the meat of an entire bull on my board, but I loaded the guests a bit lighter. We had a minimum of two loads each to take all the meat out and I wanted no sprained joints or pulled muscles among my guests or myself. I figured we could get the meat all back to the lodge in two trips each.

So a bit after dark that day we arrived at the lodge, hung the meat, enjoyed a quick dinner and a whiskey or two and went to bed.

There was no need to rush, so we all slept in. I heard some moans and groans from sore backs and shoulders but we all headed back for the final load of meat and antlers. Henry was the first to comment that had we been more patient, we likely would have had the chance to take the same caribou close to the lodge the next day. Yeah, but....

Chapter Six
A Pair Return to Trail Creek

A good number of Florida farmers have enjoyed hunts with us. The first pair came in the late 1970s and had good hunts during which each harvested a Dall ram, a moose and a caribou. They caught Arctic char and grayling near the lodge and brought in willow ptarmigan from within a half mile of camp. These fellows were not shy about telling their friends and family about their good time and we began to get more and more inquiries and guests from their circle of friends and acquaintances.

From my first guiding efforts to the present, I limited the number of people in camp to two or three hunters. We had a couple of family groups that numbered five people and once, against my advice to come in two groups of three hunters, we had six hunters in camp (more on that, later).

When hunters return to their homes they tell stories about how their trip went. It seems that those who had adverse experiences talk longer and louder about their trip. Luckily we have had few of those.

In 1996 I booked a group of three Floridians, whose story I recounted in the previous tale. Two of these men booked to come again in 1998. This time Rex was drawn for a grizzly tag.

Tom and Rex arrived on the early jet, their bags of hunting gear were found, but their rifle cases were not amidst the clutter of baggage off loaded at the Alaska Airlines ramp. We approached the desk and inquired about the whereabouts of the missing four checked pieces. The agent assured us that the pieces were in Anchorage and would arrive in Kotzebue on the afternoon flight… the afternoon of the next day!

But I had scheduled these men to travel to the lodge on the Cessna 180 flight which was to pick up three departing Dutch guests to return to Kotzebue and fly out on that evening plane. After looking over the paperwork, the station manager told us that the missing rifle cases would be sent to the lodge on a charter later than afternoon. The manager suggested that one of the men remain in town to identify the cases, then fly up on the extra charter. It made good sense.

I have always been impressed with how seldom luggage is delayed or even more rarely, lost. I was equally impressed - even more, I was surprised - with the agent's decision to pay for the charter of the cases to the lodge. That was a nine hundred dollar charter in those days.

So I stuffed the cub with what food and supplies I could, added Rex, since he had the bear permit, and we went to the lodge. The wind and weather were favorable so I sashayed around a bit in the valley looking for game. Just above the mouth of Current Creek I saw what appeared to be a grizzly feeding on a moose carcass in a dense willow thicket. What a nice way to begin a bear hunt! Then it began to rain.

Before dark, the Cessna charter landed with Tom and the missing cases. The luggage had arrived early. I had the hunters remove their rifles and send the empty hard cases back to town to store in the hanger, to minimize gear that would have to be flown out when they were completed with their hunt.

The rain became heavier and continued through the night, but it began to diminish by sunup.

Over our quick breakfast, the hunters asked me what effect the rain would have on the bear on the moose kill. I had to confess that I really didn't know, but I would bet it would have little, if any effect on the bruin. Bears wear a pretty snug raincoat - at least until we peel it off.

Trail Creek had risen a few inches, but we all got across in hip boots. We would walk up creek on the large western cutback to approach the kill site. If we proceeded slowly, the bear would not be apt to notice us. The wind was nearly calm.

We reached a spot opposite where I remembered the kill to be, but it was impossible to see anything through the dense willows. If we all concentrated on the area, someone might pick up a movement to confirm presence of the grizzly.

In anticipation of just such a prolonged period of vigilance, as we departed the lodge I had issued each of my guests a small pad to sit on. It should insulate their keisters from the cold, damp ground and keep them dry. We sat focused on that patch of brush for more than two hours. I was sure the bear would be near his food cache. A light northerly breeze developed and soon everyone felt the damp chill, in spite of their seat pads. Occasionally I would stand up and walk around some, once I did some push ups, just to warm up. My guests followed suit.

We were positioned near the mouth of Current Creek. Where that creek enters the steep canyon to the east rises a promontory which is about four hundred feet above the valley floor. On that high point lies a large boulder - a glacial erratic. Those out of place boulders tend to attract bears. This one always showed hairs on its edges due to bears scratching themselves. I had guests shoot a bear near that erratic on previous occasions.

As I traced my binocular gaze from the base to the top of the promontory, I followed a deeply worn set of foot prints, made over the centuries by grizzlies. Near the erratic boulder I saw a medium sized grizzly slowly descending the trail, following in those age-old footprints of his ancestors.

Could this be the bear I saw feeding on the moose carcass the evening before, or was it a different bruin just cruising its territory? Would it head directly to the moose carcass or disappear in the willows on the far side?

We crossed Trail Creek and remained down wind of the carcass. We had decent visibility of the tundra between the promontory and the riparian willows that held the carcass.

As we arrived at the spot from which I planned to wait for the approaching bear, it appeared, headed on a straight line for the carcass in the dense willows. It gave me the impression that it was enroute to visit its property. It exuded the aura of ownership and dominance. I doubted there was another bear on the moose kill.

I told Rex to put one up the spout and get ready. The bear continued our way, unhurriedly. At an estimated range of sixty yards I told Rex to shoot. His seven millimeter Remington struck the bear just below the throat, causing the bruin to drop in its tracks. A cleaner, more instantaneous kill I have never seen.

After photographs, I skinned the bear and removed the hams to take back to the meat pole. In

Rex and his first day grizzly.

more than thirty years of eating grizzlies from this area, only one was disagreeable in taste - we could smell the odor from that squirrel eater. After less than an hour in the oven we smelled something akin to spoiled meat mixed with poop. I threw the roast into the garbage pit and we dined on canned beef.

I wanted to take a look at the moose carcass. If it was fresh enough, I might carve off some choice cuts to dine on. That would be a small step up from road kill, but plenty fine - if fresh. If the rack was impressive I might carry it back to the lodge.

Given the possibility that another grizzly might be guarding the kill, we each stuck a round in the chamber and proceeded slowly, but we made no attempt to do so without noise. I did not want to surprise a well fed, but snoozing bear.

Apparently the bear Rex shot was the owner of this site. But I could smell spoiled meat and saw no rack of antlers. Was it a cow or calf moose? I discovered it was a large, old bull muskox. I had seen a lone male in the valley about ten days earlier and assumed this was the same animal.

The flesh would certainly not be palatable, but the massive horns were attractive to me. We were only a little over a mile from the lodge, so I planned to return with my Hudson Bay ax, remove the head and decide what to do next.

After Rex, Tom and I had a cup of fresh coffee and a short lunch, I went back for the head. I took along a large plastic bag to keep the stinking thing from contaminating my pack board. It was a shame that the beautiful hide and wonderful meat were not usable.

I had not the time nor inclination to clean up that smelly skull while at the lodge, but a few days before time to close up camp, I covered the head with salt, which immediately reduced the smell. When its came time to take it to town, I put it inside a heavy gage plastic bag, then in the back of the super cub to Kotzebue, then on my six and one half hour flight from Kotzebue to Fairbanks. Finally once in Kodiak, I boiled the head outdoors. After removing all flesh and tissue, I used a lot of forty percent hydrogen peroxide. It bleached out acceptably well.

Caribou movement through the valley was not as heavy in 1998 as usual, but we were seeing a few most days.

Never having shot a muskox, this bear kill head is in my home.

We observed a medium sized bull moose chasing a cow. The reluctant lady eventually relented to allow the amorous ungulate to have his way with her. After minimal foreplay which consisted of licking the cow's business end for a few minutes, the procreative act was quickly over in less than one minute, after which the bull dropped off her back and, head up, nose in the air, trotted away in search of another conquest. The cow just stood in place, seemingly confused or perhaps heart broken. Such is the way with too many males, it seems.

One afternoon we encountered a large porcupine. Tom bet me twenty bucks he could scratch the beast's belly. Well, for that price, I had to see his technique. I had always made it a point to keep clear of the bristle pigs and to kill any that might threaten my dogs. Since not having a Labrador in camp, I just ignore them and they wobble away. Tom used a stout walking stick to maneuver the porcupine and roll it onto its back, then he held it in place while he approached and stroked the animals belly. The porcupine seemed to be transfixed while lying on its back. It may have smiled. The show was worth the money.

Over the next four days we three traversed up and down Trail Creek without finding any "taker" caribou. On our second trip to the South Overlook I glassed a band of eight caribou up at the North Overlook and coming our way. I figured we were a good eight miles away, but the animals were coming at a fast clip, so we headed back to the eastern moguls near the lodge to intercept them.

After scrutinizing the area north of us for nearly an hour, we located the same band of bulls between Current Creek and Break Ankle Creek. They were slowly feeding as they worked their way toward us. But light was fading and no one really knows the ways of caribou, so we walked along the eastern side hill, keeping the caribou in sight as we went.

Just north of Break Ankle Creek the eight bulls went stationary, with some lying down. We had to move quickly if we were going to get a shot before dark. We dropped down into the dense willows and hurried toward the mogul the caribou were using. There were some outstanding racks in that group. I counted four that I considered possibly large enough to make the statewide top three competition. We crept our way to within a hundred and fifty yards of the resting animals.

Since Rex shot the bear and Tom had not taken anything, it was Tom's pick of the bunch. I asked each man to tell me which animal he was going to shoot, then once the first shot was placed, keep shooting the same animal until it is on the ground.

Tom's bull had a unique and outstanding rack.

Rex and his big bull with long main beams.

The two men fired almost simultaneously and two of the best bulls were lying motionless on the ground.

We would not learn until November, 1999 that the two bulls they chose would prove to place number one and number two in the annual statewide "Big 3" competition.

We had the entire next day to prepare for closing up the lodge and getting my guests, meat and trophies to Kotzebue. I took Tom and Rex to town in separate trips the next day as a new cold front arrived in northwest Alaska. Heavy snow was falling and rapidly accumulating. It was good to be out of the mountains.

The twelve days had gone by quickly with friends like Tom and Rex.

Chapter Seven
2001 Muslims Strike

Time truly flies when you're having fun. Tom Minter from Florida booked again for September, 2001.

A first cousin of mine, Steve Nason had recently been discharged from the United States Marines after serving two tours as a sniper. The young man could shoot. While he was still in grade school I threw cans for him to shoot with my iron sights .22 rifle. Within half an hour on the first afternoon of practice he was regularly hitting the cans before they touched the ground. And he had honed his marksmanship in the years since.

Both Steve and Tom had been drawn for a grizzly permit and each man was interested in pursuing caribou.

I flew my plumber friend, PlumBob, my commercial fishing and transporting partner - Tom Dooley - my sister and Tom Minter to the lodge in late August. Things had been pretty slow with a small trickle of caribou coming down the valley. It was far too warm for this time of year and maybe that was holding most of the caribou on the north slope. We had scores fo Dall sheep near the lodge but they were closed to all but local subsistence-qualified hunters.

Due to foul-ups over vacation dates at Steve's work, he would not arrive for another three days, so I took the super cub to get him. I felt guilty about departing the group in such a slow time.

On our return to the lodge we flew over a pack of eight wolves lying in the pucker brush below and across Trail Creek from the South Overlook. I made a second pass over the wolves and none even rose to stand. They appeared lazy and big bellied. Likely they had just completed a big feed. Six were grey and two were solid black.

So the plan for the next morning was set. We would go down early, and if the wolves were still in the area, we would try to kill as many as possible.

Dooley's right knee was bothering him, so with the likelihood of a ten mile or longer round trip, he elected to remain at the lodge. PlumbBob, Minter, Steve and I covered the distance to the South Overlook in three quarters of an hour.

From our prime glassing position I quickly counted all eight wolves, still basking where Steve and I saw them the previous evening. We descended from the overlook and when we reached the creek I told everyone to stick a shell in the chamber, leave the safety on, and to replace that shell in the magazine. There may be opportunities for multiple shots. I would crawl up the small cut bank with PlumbBob while Minter went up about ten yards to our right and Steve's route would be a similar distance to our left. I told each man to hold fire as long as we were closing the distance, but to shoot immediately if detected by any wolf or as soon as anyone else shot.

There was no need to designate targets, each man should shoot the nearest wolf, not worrying about the same wolf being shot by more than one man. At the sound of the first shot, the wolves would explode like popcorn out of a skillet and each hunter should shoot at will. There were at least eight lobos in the brush, and possibly more that we had not seen.

We crawled about twenty yards through the thick brush before an adult female wolf stood up about fifteen yards from us. She was nervous and looking around. I whispered to PlumbBob to shoot. The wolf went down hard and I saw several other wolves pop up within thirty yards of us. The shooting was at close range and fast. I observed one more grey drop and two black wolves seemed to be hit. In less than a minute the shooting was over. The wolves were long gone. It was too warm. We took our jackets and wind breakers off.

PlumbBob and I were only steps from the adult female grey which was stone dead, shot through the lungs.

I was certain that I saw two black wolves take a bullet, so we searched the brush for over an hour, but could not locate the carcass of either black or any more grays.

In searching the brush, I found a collar from a bear. I turned it over to the Alaska Department of Fish and Game and learned it was from a grizzly

Minter, PlumBob and Steve with the two recovered wolves.

that I had assisted in capturing alive in July, 1979 about thirty-five miles north of us. It was a seven year old, three hundred and seventy pound male at the time of capture. The collar had transmitted for about two years after placement, but that was all the information I received. That was interesting.

It's upsetting to wound and lose any animal, even a wolf. We hiked back feeling a mixture of satisfaction and disappointment. It was a sweet and sour experience.

We all walked north the next day, pausing to glass at Current Creek on the "bear stairs" - deep footprints worn into the tundra by decades or centuries of grizzlies walking up the ridge.

Max was always interested in glassing for game, often spotting animals before I did.

We walked to the North Overlook, but saw only a few ptarmigan and many Dall sheep. On the way back when we reached Current Creek I sent Steve up the bear stairs to take a peek into the valley. When he reached the top, he waved to me to join him.

Never before had I seen a moose in this valley, but we found one this day. It was a young bull, probably fifteen months of age. It would be just right for PlumbBob who told me he'd really like to take home some moose meat. I sent Steve into the valley to get upwind of the moose and drive it out into the main Trail Creek valley for PlumbBob to shoot. Packing would be much easier from there.

It worked out beautifully and the little bull came trotting out of the side valley and toward the mouth of Current Creek. One well placed neck shot from PlumbBob put the young moose on the ground. There were five of us to pack the meat out.

We each took out a big load of meat.

The next morning in drizzle and fog, we returned and packed out the rest. We were at the lodge, ready for the next act before noon.

PlumbBob, Steve and Minter with the meat bull.

Someone spotted eight caribou on the alluvial fan across the creek. Dooley, Steve and I hustled over. Dooley wanted to take one. His first shot was a miss, causing the caribou to mill around. In the confusion, Dooley shot a smaller bull. Oh well, the limit was five per day for residents and there would likely be more opportunities.

After dinner I took Dooley in the cub to look for the wolves. I found the bunch of *Canis lupus* about three miles down the creek from where the shooting took

The "bear stairs."

Steve and Dooley with Dooley's young bull.

place. This time they all started running at the sound of the aircraft. I counted only four animals and all were gray. The blacks had apparently been fatally wounded, but were lost. It's awful to loose a wounded animal, but I would have much felt worse if we saw one or both wolves still alive, but badly crippled.

Before landing I flew about six miles up the creek where Dooley and I spotted large groups of caribou coming out of the passes and headed toward the lodge. I expected to see some from the windows of the lodge by morning.

Early the next morning, September 9, we saw hundreds of caribou in large groups on east and west sides of the valley.

One bull on the west side caught my eye, so Minter and I hustled across the creek and scrambled up the cut bank to intercept the big bull. At about two hundred yards Tom began shooting. After some misses, the bull hunched up, showing he had taken a shot. I told Tom to hold his fire until we saw what the animal was going to do. In fact, the bull laid down. We were able to get to within less than one hundred yards. Tom shot again and the big bull was his.

This was an almost perfectly symmetrical rack and it scored higher than any other submitted for the statewide annual competition. It placed number one for 2001. He had previously taken a third place bull in 1996 and a first place in 1998.

The next morning Minter's luck was holding for him when using the tripod mounded spotting scope from the living room, he picked up a dark grizzly cruising through berry patches on the north facing hills near the mouth of Popple Creek, more than five miles away. He and I headed after it. We traveled down the main creek, monitoring the movements of the bear. We made good time until we came to the large patch of pucker brush - a half mile of which separated us from the bear. That tangle of "witches fingers" slowed us down, but we kept the bear in sight for most of the ninety minutes it took us to reach the area.

Minter's bull scored number one in the annual competition.

The grizzly remained focused on the abundant blue berries and with a favorable wind we were able to walk directly to a spot uphill and a hundred and twenty yards from the browsing bruin. When the bear entered a brush free spot, Minter fired. The bear erupted with a jump into the air. It bit at the site of the bullet impact and snapped at some of the bushes. Minter fired two more times.

The stricken bear charged off down hill at full speed, but after about fifty yards, it stumbled and rolled out of sight.

We took our time as we searched the brushy slope. I expected to find the bear dead, but extreme caution was in order. If the animal was wounded and mobile, it would be extremely dangerous in the tight quarters of the rock strewn, overgrown hillside.

As always in following up a wounded "brushed up" bear, I told Minter to speak loudly and often as we worked our way through the tangle of vegetation, about fifty yards apart. I wanted the bear's attention to be divided, not focused on either one of us.

We each had a cartridge in the chamber with the safety engaged.

Time flies when you're having fun, but it also passes quickly when engaged in trying to find a potentially dangerous animal in close quarters. After slowly, but noisily, moving through the ticket for half an hour, Minter

Tom Minter and his brushed up, rocked up grizzly.

hollered - "Jake, I think I see it!" I moved to stand next to Tom and yes, the hump of the well furred beast was barely perceptible about thirty yards down the hill from us. It was not moving. I threw a rock and hit the bear. It did not move.

The bear had died mid stride. Tom's first shot had penetrated both lungs. There appeared to be no more hits on the bear. It had just run out of blood and dropped. This was a good bear - a well furred boar that measured seven and a quarter feet square.

We took time to eat our sandwiches and cookies before I made the first skinning cuts. In less than two hours we had the closely fleshed hide on my pack board and were again negotiating our way through the ankle grabbing, frustrating maze of pucker brush as we headed home.

PlumbBob was scheduled to depart for Kodiak on September 10.

September 9 dawned clear and calm. Someone called "bear" which drew everyone to the windows. The huge bear in the middle of the runway had morphed into a massive bull muskox. We had a perfect opportunity to do a little photography.

The massive bovine was busy browsing on the tips of willow brush as I approached to within rock throwing distance. When I hit its rump with a baseball sized rock it wheeled around, studied me a moment, then came at me in a rush. I had seen and done this before. I turned and ran away, and after a few strides, the muskox broke off its charge.

This bull would rank high in the Boone and Crockett record book.

To my knowledge muskoxen are the only large big game animal from which one should turn and run. I have provoked single bulls on several occasions without mishap. I suspect that a group of cows with calves would circle around the calves and offer their horns to any threat, but I doubt they would attempt to charge. Maybe some day I will try that, but at the lodge, so far, we'd only seen single or pairs of old bulls, which were probably rejected from a herd.

I've never taken a muskox, but I have eaten meat given to me by friends. Some of the cuts of meat show fat marbling and overall, the meat ranks at the top of all game meat for taste.

Not being local subsistence hunters, we could only shoot this animal with cameras.

Just before dark we sighted a medium grizzly on the alluvial fan across the creek from the lodge. Steve, Dooley and I quickly went for it, but light was rapidly fading and the shooting distance was over three hundred yards so I decided we should not shoot, even considering Steve's superb marksmanship. We would hope for an opportunity earlier in the day tomorrow.

The morning dawned clear with a light south wind, but we did not sight the bear, so I decided to get PlumBob to town. Weather at Trail Creek was good for flying. The broadcast radio signal was weak, but it reported light winds for Kotzebue. With PlumbBob's moose, I had a lot of meat to get to town, so I drained five gallons from the cub's wing tanks and added about thirty additional pounds of meat. We would be heavy but within safe and comfortable performance limits of the aircraft.

We lifted off with a light wind from down the creek. The air was smooth and the ride was beautiful in brisk, clear air.

But when we reached the Noatak River, about forty miles south of the lodge, we encountered mild buffeting turbulence. I noticed that the airspeed indicator showed we were traveling at ninety-two miles per hour, but the GPS showed only sixty miles per hour. The discrepancy grew as we got closer to Kotzebue. We were dealing with strong head winds.

When I could finally hear the continual conditions broadcast, the wind in town was fifty-five gusting to sixty-two miles per hour and blowing southeast at about forty-five degrees across the north/south runway. I wished I had not removed the five gallons of gas. My super cub consumed about seven and a half gallons per hour, so I had cut our safe flying time by forty minutes!

I decided to run the right tank until the engine sputtered, then switch to the left. As we crossed the open water of the Arctic Ocean north of town I glanced at my fuel indicator gages (a small cork in a clear tube) I could see a little fuel in the left tank, but nothing showed in the right.

PlumbBob asked if I was right sure we had enough to get across the water.

"Yeah, Bob, don't worry. Right sure. Trust me." There was no place suitable for landing short of the airfield in town.

He asked, "Well what if we don't?"

"Then open the clam shell door, kick out, and swim like hell," I told him.

At five miles north I called the flight service station to tell them I intended a straight-in landing on runway 17. The dirt strip would be more forgiving in the violent wind and would allow me to land close to my tie downs. The operator gave me a wind check and said there were no other aircraft in the vicinity.

I maintained one thousand feet altitude until I was sure I could make the shore. Just as we crossed the beach, the engine sputtered. I was anticipating that and switched to the left tank. I figured I had about six minutes of fuel left. I might need a sudden burst of power to overcome adverse gusts on the ground, but I figured I had enough fuel for that.

My actual ground speed shown by the GPS was about thirty-five miles per hour when we crossed the runway threshold. I almost hovered down the strip until we were over my tie downs, then I reduced power to allow the wheels to touch the gravel, landing cross ways on the strip. Later, PlumbBob told me our touch down was imperceptible. I dumped the flaps, pushed the stick forward which brought the tail off the ground, and held the brakes as I told my passenger to get out and carefully walk to the tail of the cub, which had a hand grip. I would drop the flaps allowing the wind to push the plane back. He could steer the cub into place at my tie down spot. And that's what he did.

Before shutting down the engine, I called the flight service station to close my flight plan. The operator affirmed my message and said, "Welcome back, Jake. Nice touch down."

The big gusts were severely rocking the cub, so I hollered at PlumbBob to tie the left wing as I got out and roped off the right.

We had been in the air for two hours and twenty minutes - a hundred and forty minutes instead of the usual ninety minutes.

To my great surprise the Alaska Airlines jet came in. PlumbBob said maybe he could get on the outbound flight, so I took him directly to the terminal and he made it. As he was checking in he insisted that I keep his satellite phone, until I returned to Kodiak. At first I declined, but he insisted and I relented. That proved to be a very good thing!

After placing the meat in my freezer, and the antlers in a van, I made a quick cup of instant coffee to go and headed back to the cub with a few groceries. If conditions remained essentially the same, I would enjoy a fast trip to the lodge and be in place to hunt the next morning.

A friend came by the house to say hello and visit about the wind - to shoot the breeze, one might say. I asked if he would help me load and hold the cub until I could take off. He was happy to do so.

Each wing tank holds eighteen gallons. My electric fuel pump measured thirty five and a half gallons total to top off both tanks. I had landed with about half a gallon, or three minutes of fuel in the left tank. I always keep a small notebook handy to keep track of fuel. So far I have never run out of fuel, but this was too close!

When I called the flight service station to file a new flight plan the operator asked if I was really going to depart. Yes, I told him and I expected to return the next day. I told him I would take off directly from my tie downs, straight into the wind. That's a bit irregular but it was the best plan, given the conditions. After the jet departed there was no more planned traffic at the airport that evening.

The lightly loaded cub was airborne before I had given it full throttle. I climbed steadily and noticed at one thousand feet the air was less bumpy so I crossed the water at that altitude. Now my airspeed indicator showed ninety-two miles per hour and the GPS showed we were traveling at one hundred thirty miles an hour over the terrane. Enroute I was showing even faster ground speed. Instead of the usual ninety minutes to the lodge I arrived after only fifty-five minutes. That was like money in the bank! When I arrived it was blowing only about fifteen miles per hour from down creek - the south - at the lodge.

Minter told me he should depart the next morning to make his connections to Florida. I told him we would check the wind and weather. I was not going to remove any fuel for the next trip.

Once Minter was gone, we would concentrate on finding a good caribou and grizzly for Steve. He had been patient.

Over coffee the next morning the Kotzebue broadcast radio was not readable. After the previous day's surprise wind, I called the flight service station using PlumbBob's satellite phone. The call was immediately transferred to Fairbanks. A highly excited operator told me that America was under attack. New York City, Washington D.C. and some place in Pennsylvania had been attacked. All civilian aviation flights, including jets, were grounded until further notice. We were under wartime rules. I gave the attendant my aircraft number, N3421P, and told him to close my flight plan.

Everyone heard my conversation and all were dumbfounded. Minter broke the silence saying, "Jake, this ain't no joke. I watched your face, the attack is real, buddy!"

My sister Pat made some pancakes and Dooley fiddled with the broadcast radio receiver, eventually picking up a faint, barely understandable voice. We took turns trying to hear the news.

I called Kodiak to tell my wife, Teresa, to not allow our two daughters to attend school until I gave her the okay. If the terrorists were highly organized and had truly invaded our country, attacks in rural communities would spread the panic - serving the terrorists well. I wanted to take no chances with our kids' safety.

If I hadn't returned to the lodge in that big wind, I would have been marooned in Kotzebue for the next three days.

About 10am, Pat spotted a large grizzly on the hillside across East Bowl Creek and coming our way. I told Steve to get ready, Minter wanted to come along so I told him to do so.

But first, I wanted to be sure my flight plan was closed. I called the Kotzebue station again and this time got an old hand who was calm and collected. I closed the plan a second time.

Pat and Dooley tried to keep track of the bear, but they would lose sight of it from time to time. Once Steve, Tom and I were on the ground we could not see it. I took us down the runway and to the mouth of East Bowl Creek. We got on a small knoll to glass. We soon found the bear in the east moguls, munching on berries but gradually working its way closer toward the lodge.

We eased through the riparian growth on the north side of East Bowl Creek and reached the foothills of the mogul formation. I noticed that a flag was up on the east side of the lodge. In that same binocular view the big grizzly showed the top of its back as it ambled along. We moved closer until the bear stood up on its hand legs - an uncommon event - and at two hundred yards, Steve center punched it in the brisket. The bear dropped dead as a rock.

This was a dandy buff colored bear of over eight feet square - larger than the average we take.

Dooley and Pat joined us and let us know they had put the flag up not for this bear, but for another large one that had been in the yard next to the three wheelers. Where it went they did not know.

We'd all forgotten to eat any lunch, so we had a big meal of caribou, potatos, salad and fresh blue berry pie. It had been quite a day .... but at six in the evening, it wasn't yet over.

With two buckets in hand I went for fresh water. As I was ready to enter the lodge I heard the wump, wump, wump of a large helicopter coming up the valley.

Dooley popped the window open and hollered, "Partner (he's from

2001 Muslims Strike

Steve Nason and his dandy grizzly on 9/11. The lodge is visible over Steve's left shoulder. He called it the Bin Laden Bear.

Everyone helped celebrate Steve's grizzly.

This robust, healthy boar grizzly had the worst infestation of gut round worms I've seen.

Alabama and pronounces it "Phodna") they's a black helicopter coming at us and theys rocket pods on both sides.

I rushed inside to get a look at what was coming, grabbed my .44 pistol and told everyone to grab their rifles and ammunition and get well away from the building. If we were going to be attacked, the building would be the first target.

The large black chopper was hovering near the lodge when my guests came boiling out of the building. I did not see any identifying insignia on the ominous appearing war machine.

The helicopter abruptly turned and set down at the far end of the runway.

My Honda three wheeler started on the first pull and I headed for the helicopter with my headlight on. Steve jogged behind and set up in prone position with his rifle on the near end of the runway.

With engine running, an apparently unarmed man in military camouflage got out of the chopper and walked my way. I stopped my machine midway down the eleven hundred foot main runway.

"What's your name?" I hollered when the soldier was fifty yards from me.

"Olanna, Sir. Are you Jacobson?, was his reply.

So, you're from Shishmaref - what are you doing here?" I asked.

"My Dad's from Shishmaref. I'm from the National Guard in Nome and we're here to make sure you are all right, he said.

He came to me, offering to shake hands.

"That chopper has no identifying insignia. If you were wearing a turban, my cousin would have shot your head off," I assured him. "Why the hell don't you have a bull horn for an operation like this? Especially on a day like this." I was frazzled and angry.

We shook hands and I invited him and the crew to come up for a piece of fresh pie.

He told me that his pilot didn't like what he saw developing, so he withdrew. He said they would be returning to Nome.

Darkness was closing on the country, but that helicopter could easily handle night flight, nevertheless Olanna told me they would return to base. He asked if we needed anything.

I told him we were nearly out of whiskey. He reported they had no booze aboard.

I asked for an update on the attacks on our country, but he said he knew nothing more than he did when they departed Nome. He mentioned that officers in the Nome detachment felt they should just do something, and elected to check on me because my lodge was in such a beautiful location.

Cooled down, I offered to bring a thermos of coffee to send with them, but Olanna said they were well supplied. I wished him a safe flight back to Nome. He thanked me and returned to the helicopter whereupon the machine lifted off and flew down the valley without passing over the lodge.

Back at the lodge it seemed like time for a whiskey for everyone from our diminished supply. What a day this had been! What's coming next?

We strained to hear the faint radio signal, which broadcast the often updated report on events of the day and emphasized that all civilian flight was forbidden. We were under wartime rules.

We understood that muslim terrorists had commandeered several commercial passenger jets and flown some planes into major buildings including the World Trade Center in New York and the Pentagon in Washington, D.C. Thousands of Americans had been killed in this sneak attack. Pennsylvania was attacked. Coming to terms with the fact that our country had been so horribly attacked by malevolent muslims would take some time. We were all shocked.

The radio reception was still scratchy and difficult to hear the next morning, which dawned clear and calm. Civilian flight was still not allowed in rural Alaska.

We could not have hoped for a better place in which to be grounded and isolated due to the attack. We all headed north after breakfast. About mid afternoon we found a decent caribou for Steve just north of the mouth of Current Creek. The lone bull was munching on lichens as he ambled down the valley. Steve and I easily moved into position to intercept the animal and one shot from Steve's heavy barreled .300 Winchester magnum put the bull on the ground, motionless. The bullet impacted just behind the head.

After age seven, most caribou racks begin to diminish in overall size and the number of projection points. Normally I hold off on having guests shoot caribou with less than seven projection points in the upper part of each antler, but this bull had longer than normal main beams and was esthetically pleasing. Also, caribou herd movements can begin and end abruptly. We'd had several days of good selection, but that might be nearing an end. We also did not know when we would hear that civilian flight was approved, to allow us to depart for town. Both Steve and Minter were already several days late returning home.

It was an older bull. The teeth were badly worn and the antlers gave me the impression that this animal was past its prime.

This was the largest bodied caribou the season, so Steve and I each packed out half of the animal. Its tenderloins with fried eggs made a grand breakfast for all the next morning.

Cousin Steve with his big, old bull.

The radio continued to sputter out static bursts of information on the confusing situation, as the federal government dealt with the terrorist attacks.

With time on our hands, Steve and Tom got in some stream fishing for Arctic char and grayling, while Dooley and I built a shelf for additional pot and pan storage in the kitchen area. We added a hand rail to the stairs, cut wood for the sauna, and did a few other minor things.

It was great that I had PlumbBob's satellite phone. I called every morning to see when I could take first Steve, who had an employer, then Tom, who was self-employed, to town.

On Wednesday afternoon, September 13, the Federal Aviation Administration announced that civilian flight was allowed, but I did not get that information until too late to make the flight to Kotzebue.

First thing Thursday morning I called the Kotzebue flight service station and got the okay, so I filed a flight plan. Weather was good and meteorological winds were light, unlike the political winds gusting through our country and the world.

Temperatures had remained just below freezing. The meat hanging on the pole had formed a dark, almost black crust. It had aged wonderfully. No sign nor odor of spoilage or fly blow was found.

Minter and Steve. Both took good caribou trophies.

After loading Steve, his bear skin, and as much meat into the cub as I could safely transport, we were ready. I did not remove any fuel for this trip. I tied his caribou rack on one wing strut and Minter's on the other side. It was time to go to town.

Our trip was unremarkable and we landed in just under ninety minutes. As I was refueling, Steve removed the caribou racks and unloaded the meat.

An Alaska Airlines pilot, named Tom, who I had known for many years came by to tell me that his bother-in-law was the helicopter pilot who flew the chopper to Trail Creek. This fellow told me that he had been told that in Nome, the National Guard commander felt he just had to do something, so he sent the helicopter up to check on our welfare. He said that whole operation was an unnecessary fiasco. He also told me that his relative was concerned when he saw us departing the lodge with rifles in hand, that his aircraft might soon be taking fire.

Steve told him that he was planning to shoot the tail rotor if I gave the order, or if the situation turned aggressive.

We had a short laugh, but this was not a laughing matter.

I promised to contact the National Guard to complain that the helicopter did not have a bull horn and had no markings to identify it. On a day like September 11, 2001, these were dangerous omissions.

Off to town, late but legal.

After putting the meat and bear hide in the freezer, I dropped Steve at the Alaska Airlines terminal to book his flight and headed back up for Minter.

This was an efficient, inconsequential round trip. Minter was ready and Dooley had a big load of meat ready to go to town.

Minter and I landed and were soon joined by Steve who had secured a seat out on the next evening jet. Minter was able to get a ticket for the same flight. We ate hamburgers at a local greasy spoon and called it a day.

Air freight out of Kotzebue was backlogged by at least a week, but Steve was able to mail his caribou rack to Arizona. The two bear skins got sealed and documented by the Alaska Department of Fish and Game and remained in my freezer until they could be safely shipped by frozen air freight.

After the pair were checked in I headed back up to get Pat and a load of meat. A new four inch covering of snow showed no sign of caribou movement. Having Steve shoot his bull may have been the last opportunity for collecting one this season.

The hour was late and visibility was reduced to a quarter of a mile in snow so I stayed the night. Visibility remained below safe minimums until after noon the next day.

Kotzebue radio was giving 5 miles visibility and forecast a large storm to come in the next night, so I loaded Pat and several hundred pounds of prime meat and delivered both to the cabin in Kotzebue, then turned around to get Dooley and Max, my Labrador.

Weather was deteriorating which forced me to follow the still unfrozen stream of Trail Creek into camp. Dooley had the remainder of the meat ready to load, but when I landed, I had to use brakes and the big tires picked up and slung rocks behind. One of the rocks struck the lower right brace for the horizontal stabilizer. The metal attaching tab had broken at the fuselage. The heavy wire brace was hanging from its upper attachment. It would not be safe to fly this way.

By incredibly good luck, there was enough of the attachment tab which extended from the lower longeron to drill a new hole and reattach the safety brace.

Trail Creek valley looked different the morning of September 16.

We brought my old Sears 1500 watt generator (which I had been using since 1969) and a drill and soon had the brace re-installed.

With visibility reduced to half a mile in snow, and darkness coming on, Dooley, Max and I said good-bye to Trail Creek and headed for home.

We landed about forty minutes after dark without problems. That was about how much time repair of the brace had taken.

This twelve day booking had been extended three days due to the muslim terrorist attacks and another couple of days due logistics. But, among other things, we had taken one moose, five caribou, two grizzlies, two wolves, and made some unforgettable memories.

It had been the most truly unique booking period I had seen in my past twenty-nine years of guiding hunters in rural Alaska.

That so many things could take place in such a short period of time gives me pause for reflection. But then, hunting is often like that.

I doubt that I will ever again experience such an action-packed, unique series of events.

One just can't make up stuff like this!

Sister Pat and me with nice Kings. Daughter Kate looks awestruck.

Chapter Eight

At Trail Creek, 2002

On Monday, August 19 I made final preparations for heading up north to begin the guided hunts. Weather was beautiful in Kodiak with 51 degrees and light winds. I loaded our 1999 Ford pickup canopy with freight items to be shipped from Fairbanks, emergency gear for the flight from Fairbanks to Kotzebue and necessities for use during the time I spent in Fairbanks getting the annual inspection completed on the super cub. I filled a large icebox with eighty pounds of frozen halibut and salmon to share with friends along the way.

King salmon trolling was in full swing and we were making good catches close to the house, making departure a regrettable necessity.

The ferry *F/V Tustumena* departed on time at 10:30 that evening. I enjoyed having a stateroom in which to sleep during the journey to Homer, where I offloaded the truck at nine o'clock in heavy fog and no wind. I was in Anchorage by 1:00pm. The two hundred fifty miles of road to Anchorage was plugged with tourist motor homes and vehicles, as is usual for that time of year. I was thankful that Kodiak does not have a road connection which would bring in droves of visitors every summer. As it is, we already have one traffic light and road congestion is far more noticeable than it was twenty years ago. Give me back the poorly maintained dirt roads with no lights and fewer people!

The big box stores in Anchorage provided me with many food items at prices far below those found in Kodiak or Kotzebue. After three hours of shopping in amongst the crowds of Anchorage (Anguish I call it) I delivered some fish to friends and then drove the 304 miles to Fairbanks in four and a half hours due to light traffic and fewer motor homes. At Chena Marina I parked next to the cub which appeared to have wintered well. I got in the back with the freight and immediately went to sleep. It had been a good day.

Wednesday and Thursday I did most of the work for the annual, all except the compression check which my mechanic friend Jimmy Anderson did. All cylinders passed, so I flew five practice take off and landings and was ready to fly the 440 miles to Kotzebue, when weather permitted.

Friday I was ready to depart, but the battery, which was only two years old wouldn't turn the engine over so I drove across town and bought a new one. The weather had come down a little, but I got a "Special" to depart the control zone and flew at less than a thousand feet to Nenana where the ceiling lifted. Enroute I was able to cruise at 7,500 to Kotzebue. After only five and a half hours bunched up in the cub, I landed in Kotzebue.

Some stranger was in my tie down spot, so I rounded up some old tires and dug in three new tie downs. The sod shack in Kotzebue was a mess, as usual. The chest freezer had been left unplugged by the renter with meat and fish inside, making a stinking hole of it. I went to bed, feeling disgusted with inconsiderate people about midnight.

Saturday I went to my daughter Sandy's for breakfast then spent the day cleaning out the freezer and the shack in general. By evening I had the freezer reasonably clean and cold enough for me to put my frozen items inside. I loaded the cub with food and other freight and landed at the lodge at 9:30pm. It was +58 degrees in light southerly wind. I found no bear damage, but a can of root bear left on the table had frozen, then exploded, leaving a sticky residue all over.

Sunday began nice with a high overcast and south wind at fifteen knots. Over my coffee I glassed sheep on both sides of the creek. Heavy, muddy caribou trails confirmed passage of thousands a month or so earlier.

After servicing and starting both Honda 110 three wheelers, I put out the red cones marking the two runways, hung up the wind flag, and cut the willows that had grown enough to obscure vision from the lodge windows.

The dip water hole was cleared of branches and leaves, as was the bathing pool by the sauna.

I grilled a slab of salmon outside and enjoyed that and some Top Ramen for lunch and dinner. I daydreamed of Zeke and Max, my labs. I missed them.

Monday I planned to return to Kotzebue to visit the National Park Service superintendent, talk with the Alaska Department of Fish and Game and do more cleaning at the shack. I was unable to get the Satellite Phone to connect, so with visibility of half a mile, I took off about two that afternoon and found better conditions from midway to town and the rest of the way.

My 1977 Ford pickup refused to start, so I got a jump and put a trickle charger on it. I had supper with my son, Martin and his wife, Momsy.

Tuesday was the primary election. I had voted absentee. My good friend Wayne Ross was running against U.S. Senator Murkowski for governor, but recognition and being part of the establishment prevailed, so Murko won. Sarah Palin, who I had know for several years was running a bit behind Loren Lehman for Lieutenant Governor. My friend from Wasilla, Alaska State Representative Scott Ogan kept his seat. It seemed that overall conservative Republicans had done reasonably well.

On Thursday August 29, as I was about to take off with my first guest, Dick, a Federal Aviation inspector from Fairbanks came to my cub as the engine was warming up and announced he was doing a ramp inspection.

I shut down the engine and followed him around as he scrutinized control services, cables, brakes, and engine. All passed, but he noticed that my flying charts were outdated - some by several years. The charts are just maps and geography does not change much, nevertheless he demanded that I update all my charts. Also he told me that the "Supplement" book was not required, but it's a violation to have an outdated one. What baloney! No aviation charts were available at the flight service station in Kotzebue, so I ordered some from Fairbanks and took off for Trail Creek.

After getting Dick situated I returned to Kotzebue to meet PlumbBob and Janet (aka Tundra Plumb). They had been delayed and would come the next day. I encountered some surprise headwinds of thirty knots or so, but the wind in town was only eighteen knots. I got with a friend who had also flown for Leon Shellabarger and practiced up on doing weight and balance calculations for the cub, in case the inspector returned and demanded one.

The next day I took PlumbBob to the lodge, then Janet. Flying was VFR on top for the trip with Janet. Heavy fog and rain had moved in reducing visibility to less than a mile. The remains of a typhoon from the

Philippines had arrived in northwest Alaska and kept the entire region wet and uncomfortable for the five days Janet had allotted to spend with us.

This year, for the first time in nearly a decade, all cow moose I observed were accompanied by one or two calves. I wasn't doing a thorough survey, but I usually saw plenty of moose on trips to and from town. The extraordinarily high grizzly population was credited with consuming the moose calves within their first month of life. The moose population had been going downhill for the past ten years. In other parts of Alaska restrictions on size of bulls legal to harvest, drawing permits and residency requirements were already imposed and would likely come to northwest Alaska. The Alaska Department of Fish and Game was way behind the curve on this.

But so far I had been seeing fewer bears on Trail Creek than normal. The berry crop is key to bear numbers and our berries this season were not abundant. The grizzlies' favorite - the high bush soap berries -were fewest in number that I had ever noticed. I suspect the bears prefer these appropriately named berries because they can browse through the bushes stripping the little red fruits from the branches without bending over. The awful tasting berries may have a role in forming the grizzly personality.

We got a break in the weather on opening day of grizzly season, which was September 1 in those days. We four walked north to the "bear stairs" on Currant Creek to glass. Soon Dick or I spotted buff colored bear feeding near the mouth of MacKenzie Pass, a mile and a half from us. The bruin was covering ground rapidly in its back and forth search for calories, so we left PlumbBob and Janet and humped up the drainage, then across the main channel, as fast as we could go.

The broken small hills and lack of wind made for ideal stalking, allowing us to go directly to within a hundred and fifty yards of the preoccupied animal. When Dick squeezed his trigger the bear jumped straight up with all feet off the ground, and came to earth on its belly. The medium sized boar never knew what hit him. It was a heart shot.

After carefully skinning the beast to avoid packing unnecessary weight, I removed the gall bladder and looked around the abdominal cavity. I found that Dick's bullet had pierced the heart dead center. I've seen heart-shot animals rear up and go over backward, but most take off on a dead run for about fifty yards. This bruin's reaction was less common in my experience.

At Trail Creek, 2002

Dick and his opening day "dish-faced" grizzly.

Dick had been with me when Greg Fischer was badly mauled by a bear two years before. He had helped get Greg back to the lodge from the site of the attack four and a quarter GPS miles downstream, so we had some reminiscing to do as we hiked the five miles back to the lodge. This time we were able to avoid water deeper than the top of our knee boots. We were all soaked with boots full of water when we got Greg to the lodge.

Before we reached our shelter the wind and rain had resumed.

Janet had prepared a big dinner and we wolfed it down as the driving rain noisily pummeled the building.

The continuous downpour brought the creeks up quickly. The day after Dick shot his bear we would not have been able to cross the main channel of Trail Creek.

We had each other's good company, books, cards and pleasant indoor conditions, but outside it was miserable for the next two days. I recall periods like this spent in wall tents which are no comparison to a solid building. Janet decided that she should go to town as soon as conditions permitted, as she had appointments to keep in Anchorage.

So on September 4 I loaded Janet, Dick's bear skin and some miscellaneous stuff that I had waiting for a less than full plane to town. That trip was a turbulent pounder all the way to Kotzebue. But we arrived safely and she made it out on the evening jet. I returned to the lodge.

One evening conditions partially lifted. We three had just finished dinner and poured a whiskey. Dick went to the outhouse and as I washed

PlumbBob Johnson and the young meat moose.

the dishes PlumbBob spotted a meat moose in the low widows off the end of the runway and across the creek. I threw my binoculars up and asked PlumbBob if he wanted to take it. He answered affirmatively.

Apparently something had buggered the young bull as it was trotting, then walking, then breaking into a trot again. There was no time to get Dick, who would not have been interested in the meat anyway. PlumbBob and I rushed down stairs, pulled on our hip boots and jogged to intercept the oncoming young bull.

The river was high but a diagonal series of riffles indicated a fordable path across. We crossed and a few yards from a dense stand of willows. PlumbBob dropped the moose. I snapped a quick photograph and sent PlumbBob back for our packboards and a short ax for the ribs, while I began removing quarters. With the rain I would leave the hide on the leg pieces until later.

This animal was sporting its first, or possibly second set of antlers. Its body was comparatively small as well. I was already tasting the wonderful meat. Normally I keep half the usable meat of animals we take on guided trips. Half a moose each fall, along with other wild game meat makes store-bought meat a rare thing in our house.

PlumbBob returned with Dick and one three-wheeler and trailer. We had the animal across the creek and at the meat pole in about an hour and a half. Those whiskey's would go neglected no longer!

Rain resumed and continued until time for PlumbBob to depart. We removed the skin from the quarters and loaded Bob's half of the meat into the cub, he caught a jet to Anchorage the next morning. That same flight brought in a friend from Kodiak, Tom Emerson.

Emerson had done a lot of welding on my fishing boat in Kodiak and never charged me enough, so I told him either I would go to the bank to draw some cash and stick in his pocket or I would buy him a ticket to Kotzebue for a spell of hunting. He was happy to accept the trip.

Weather was down again. Rain mixed with snow made for reduced visibility. We had to wait until after 1:00pm to depart for the lodge. Once we were out of the control zone I few low level, following the channels of open water into the mountains. It was a touchy-feely trip and took nearly two hours instead of the normal ninety minutes.

Five miles south of the lodge I began seeing trails in the new fallen snow indicative of the passage hundreds of caribou, maybe more. Visibility at the camp was about half a mile.

We landed, but Dick was not there. After securing the aircraft and packing our stuff to the lodge, Dick came walking through the willows with blood on his hands. He had filled his two caribou tags, but he was not sure where the carcasses were. The visibility was that bad. Tom and I went to the east moguls with Dick and located the two gutted bulls. They were difficult to find in the salt and pepper snow cover.

Both were older, mature bulls in robust condition. Prime table fare! We had them both packed to the meat pole in less than an hour.

ALASKA CARIBOU

Dick with his first caribou.

Dick's second bull. The lodge is visible over his right shoulder.

It was good that Dick took the initiative and dropped those caribou. We had seen only singles and scattered groups of cows, calves and young bulls. A fall storm like the one we had been enduring for the past week and now turned to snow, sometimes motivates caribou to depart the North Slope in massive herds which keep going until they are beyond our reach.

Tom Emerson's main interest was in shooting some willow ptarmigan with a shotgun an old friend had recently given him. But like most of us,

At Trail Creek, 2002

when he saw the magnificent bull caribou, he wanted to collect one. He did not bring a rifle, but I keep a spare .300 Winchester magnum at the lodge.

Snow fell throughout the night and was still coming down at day break. We were in the midst of a white-out. By the look of the trails in the deepening snow, thousands of animals had passed by the lodge during the night.

We enjoyed a hearty breakfast of eggs, caribou tenderloins and toast, with coffee when I noticed a band of seventeen large antlered bulls coming our way through the cotton-white conditions along the eastern side hill.

Tom's neck shot dropped the magnificent animal in its tracks.

This group of caribou was approaching at a rapid pace, so Tom and I pulled on our hip boots, grabbed our rifles and headed across the still unfrozen swamp for the moguls. In my haste, I forgot to put on the white camouflage parkas which I kept hanging handy near the stove.

We didn't have long to wait. Just as we reached a convenient ditch to conceal our approach, the first of the group of seventeen appeared fifty yards from us, headed south. At the end of the string of bulls was the one I wanted Tom to take. It was large in body and carried a rack that set it apart from its herd mates. It clearly was a bull for the record books. It has always seemed strange to me that the biggest bulls are usually found walking at the tail end of a group, but it is consistently the case.

Tom lined up with my loaner rifle and stuck a hundred and fifty grain guided missile in the bull's neck. The animal dropped mid-stride and did not move.

My first thought was I wish every hunter was granted an opportunity to take a capital animal like this one. Dick joined us, offered heartfelt congratulations and helped us cut up and pack the meat.

Dick regretted his airline flight schedule which had him departing Kotzebue on the evening flight of the next day. If visibility improved I would fly him to town this afternoon, if not, we would see what the morning offered.

Now we were seeing primarily older bulls and the groups were smaller, with dozens, rather than hundreds of animals. I sensed that the caribou might soon be long gone to the south. The resident bag limit was five caribou and I wanted some meat. Tom was willing to shoot two more, but we found no more trophy class critters. Late that afternoon with snow still falling, two mature meat bulls were added to the meat pole. At sundown I could see better conditions to the south of us. It was eighteen degrees above zero, so I put the catalytic heater in the engine cowling and tied down the engine cover.

Tom and his ptarmigan.

Something woke me up about two in the morning. I went to the window to look at the meat pole, but saw nothing, however I did see stars. It looked like a good day coming. The temperature was twenty-five degrees above zero, warmer than I had anticipated, and there was little wind.

After breakfast I loaded Dick and his gear along with the last of the moose meat and some caribou meat and headed for Kotzebue.

In town I learned that hunting had been slim throughout most of the region. So, it seemed we had done pretty well, considering all.

At Trail Creek, 2002

Tom holding his first Arctic Char.

Tom and another bunch of ptarmigan and two of his caribou racks.

Dick got his gear and antlers checked in. This was his second trip to hunt with me and I told him I hoped he would come again.

It was twenty-eight degrees in Kotzebue, so after topping off the freezer I put the rest of the meat in a van, fueled the cub and went back up to Tom.

It had warmed up to thirty-four degrees when I landed. My friend Tom had caught and released some fresh Arctic char and shotgunned a nice mess of willow ptarmigan - which is all he actually came for. We had enough birds for a nice meal and two packages to take home. His wife had never eaten this variety of "wild chicken." That would be a real treat for her.

But with time enough for a short walk to the main channel of Trail Creek, I wanted a photo of Tom with an Arctic Char, so with one rifle, a shotgun and one fishing pole, we struck off.

Tom was from Kodiak where fishing is close at hand nearly everyday. After catching and releasing several medium-sized Char, Tom headed for a large flock of ptarmigan which had just landed nearby. These birds would be in prime eating condition, unlike the Char which had traveled a couple hundred miles without eating in their spawning run.

The elevation of the lodge is 1,380 feet. Snow was melting fast at the lower levels. We had been blessed with great hunting and comfortable conditions, but it was time to close up the lodge until next summer. The next morning we loaded the last of the meat. Tom rode with two caribou hinds in his lap.

Everything went well, Tom caught the morning jet to return to Kodiak with his caribou rack and meat for both of us. That caribou placed number two in the annual statewide competition. That's pretty good for a ptarmigan hunt, I'd say.

Chapter Nine

2003 Return of the Maneater

In 2003 to hunt grizzly bears in northwest Alaska, non-residents had to be drawn for a permit. Drawings are a huge pain in the neck for guides, but the law must be followed. Over the past several years, the number of applicants had sometimes been fewer than the number of permits available, so left over permits could be awarded on request, but not until after the drawing which took place in late May. Alaska residents could take a grizzly without a drawn permit.

Dall sheep hunting was closed in my area to all but subsistence qualified local residents. No non-residents were allowed to hunt sheep, due to federal subsistence regulations.

Initially moose regulations allowed for any antlered bull to be taken. With the newly permitted influx of large numbers of Transported, non-guided, or dropped off hunters, the moose population had been severely depleted in my area.

I stopped booking guests specifically for moose hunts in 1998.

Ten or fifteen years too late, the Alaska Department of Fish and Game finally required that non-residents take moose with a minimum of fifty-five inches in antler width or four brow tines on at least one side.

Beginning in 1998, for guests wanting to take a moose, I suggested they apply for a permit, the application only cost $5.00. If they were drawn for a permit and purchased a metal locking tag, they could harvest a moose if we found one during the pursuit of other animals. They could use the moose tag on other animals for which the tag cost the same or less than a moose, such as caribou for which the annual bag limit was 5 animals. Prior to the heavy harvest of moose and depletion of the population, my guests had done exceptionally well in taking huge moose, but the potential for a great bull was low by 2003. I did not encourage moose hunters to come with me.

So, I focused on the pursuit of grizzly, caribou, wolves, and wolverine on opportunity. I reminded everyone that guests opportunities to take a wolverine rarely occurred.

It was a lean year. My bookings were fewer than I would have liked, due to the restrictions, but my friend, a guide from Wyoming named Greg Fischer, had been awarded a grizzly permit. (Greg had been almost fatally mauled by a grizzly on Trail Creek in 2000.) I had made permit applications for two men from South Africa and one had been successful. Three residents from Kodiak were booked to come to hunt caribou and wolves.

Summer in Kodiak is always over too soon. We had been enjoying excellent trolling for King and Silver salmon as well as bait fishing for halibut. We had plenty of prime fish for our needs and surplus to share with friends. I packed a large cooler full of halibut to take to Kotzebue where the water contains no large flatfish, making halibut a rare delicacy.

A decent day of family halibut fishing, tough to tear away from to go north.

On August 18 I boarded the *F/V TUSTUMENA* and slept in my stateroom on the way to Homer. Staterooms on that boat are more like jail cells, but they do have reasonable beds.

The trip to Fairbanks followed Costco shopping in Anchorage and delivery of fish to friends. When I arrived at Windy Pass, feeling sleepy, I pulled off the road and napped for an hour, then headed north.

The annual inspection went quickly this time and I flew the five take-offs and landings shortly after 3pm on Wednesday, August 20. Things were going very efficiently. I spent the night in my mechanic, Jimmy Anderson's little log cabin and slept well.

Thursday morning was a bit foggy but decent in Fairbanks, however visibility in Tanana was a quarter of a mile in fog. In looking over the charts at the flight service station, I figured I could get out of town, then go "VFR on top" until I found a hole somewhere west of half the distance to Kotzebue. I would have to buck a fifteen mile per hour wind from the west, but that was better than hanging around in Fairbanks. The outlook for improvement was not good.

I wove my way to 8,500 feet and stayed there for most of the trip. The air was pretty smooth with little turbulence. One hundred miles east of Kotzebue I could hear VHF radio traffic and the nondirectional beacon broadcasts giving marginal conditions. I augured down to twelve hundred feet and went "touchy feely" the rest of the way. The trip took six and a half hours, not much over normal time for the 440 miles.

My decrepit 1977 pickup took some fussing to start, but I got it going by taking off the air cleaner and pouring raw gas directly into the carburetor. The sod shack was in decent condition this time and the freezer was cold, clean, and empty. Several friends came by to say hello. I was in bed by 11:00pm.

Friday morning I hooked up my local telephone, filled my gas trailer with 400 gallons of 100 octane and took it to the airplane. I stopped by to pick up a left over grizzly tag for the South African guest.

Our daughters, Bess and Kate, were coming up on the same jet flight that Rob Coyle, my assistant guide was using, but they needed to have passports to fly without a parent. It took four phone calls with my wife, Teresa, coaching her through opening the combination of the gun safe where the passports were secured. Finally she got the safe open. She'd never done that before.

Rob and the girls arrived the next morning. I sent Rob, Bess, Kate and two grandsons, Spencer and Stuart, to the lodge on a Cessna 206 charter. When I started off for the lodge I noticed low oil pressure, so I returned. When I opened the cowling and took off the oil pressure spring housing I found a small piece of carbon near the port. I cleaned the carbon out and restarted. The oil pressure returned to normal.

Upon landing the kids excitedly all told me about a large grizzly that came running at them shortly after the charter plane left. Spencer fired two times and the bear ran back. Rob said it was a big grizzly.

In light rain, the next morning Rob took the boys up the creek. The girls helped me patch a couple of small leaks in the shop roof and other minor chores before we went fishing. Ravens peck the gravel from the rolled roofing which causes leaks.

They love to fish and each caught some grayling and Arctic char for dinner.

It had been several years since the buildings were last stained, so I spent the day getting the first coat on the three buildings.

Bess and Kate prepared lunches and the evening meal, including a Dutch oven cake. In the afternoon they had time for some kite flying.

Rob spotted a good ram in the east bowl, so he and Spencer went for it. The stalk and approach were straightforward and the two were back at the lodge in three and a half hours.

It seems that anytime big government gets involved with making things more "fair," or in favoring one group of citizens over others, the well intentioned plans are thwarted by actions of those supposedly favored.

A Kotzebue school teacher with a super cub qualified for subsistence sheep hunting due to his living there. The previous season he had taken rams for himself, his wife, and as "proxy hunter" for two members of his church - four rams! This was clearly abuse, and the federal government reacted by requiring that the trophy value of any animals harvested under subsistence regulation, be destroyed. So, due to the new regulations, Spencer had to surrender the horns of his sheep to the Alaska Department of Fish and Game, where they sawed off one horn. At least he and Rob enjoyed the hunt. We all enjoyed the meat.

Spencer's second old ram was similar to his first taken two years before.

The next day I rolled a second coat of stain on the buildings while the girls puttered around, cleaning up and such. Then we had another round of stream fishing, this was a catch and release day.

Rob had the boys up creek were Stuart shot a lone cow caribou at about seventy-five yards. It was his first big game animal.

About three that afternoon I flew to Kotzebue to meet four incoming guests. All arrived on the evening flight. Three had reservations for rooms at the NuLukVik Hotel, while Greg Fischer would stay with me. At ten the next morning the three from Kodiak were on the Cessna charter to the lodge. That same plane brought the four kids and fresh meat back. I took Greg up that evening.

The preliminaries were done and now the booked hunts would begin.

Everybody sighted in their rifles and after a few drinks, all hit the sack.

August 31 brought good weather and hundreds of caribou ambling about on both sides of the valley. The animals looked like they moved in to stay, but of course, they would soon move on.

PlumbBob and Greg went with me and each shot a medium bull on the west side of the valley. Rob took Grant and Barry along the southeast side of Trail Creek. Each guest planned to take two caribou, so they were

Greg and his first bull. Fall colors are coming out.

not overly selective on their first ones. At the end of the first day, we had four bull caribou on the meat pole.

September 1 was opening day of grizzly season. I was making coffee when I noticed that our meat pole had been visited. Several quarters were missing. As I gazed out the window, movement from a light colored object caught my eye. Across East Bowl Creek and headed into a swale choked with thick willows was a light colored grizzly. Rob was out of his bed in the upstairs pantry in time to see the critter disappear into the brush. We were lucky to see it. It was more than a half mile from the lodge, but I figured it was the one that visited us last night.

As pretty a grizzly as they get. And a hunter as happy as they get.

Over coffee I told everyone that I expected the bruin to make a bed in the willows and remain there for most of the day. It may stand up to pee or poop, as healthy bears do not mess their own nests. If we are in position we might see it then and make a stalk. If not, then late in the afternoon I expected it to come back for more meat snacks.

Before we all headed up to the eastern moguls, I put a large turkey in the oven and left it on 300 degrees. I filled a small thermos with

2003 Return of the Maneater

PlumbBob, Rob and Greg with the beautiful boar grizzly.

Greg is reminiscing about his mauling that took place in September 2000.

coffee for the fellows to sip as we waited. A new skiff of snow showed on the peaks.

We all put on an extra layer as the north wind was penetrating and cold.

Our group of six settled in to wait and watch, but after two hours in the bitter wind shivering, I decided to change plans. We could adequately stake out the thicket in shifts. I would take the first watch, then in two hours a couple of guys could come and take over. If the bear showed, one of the watchers should hustle to the lodge to get Greg to shoot it.

As it turned out my first shift lasted for over four hours. I did push-ups and stomped my feet to keep warm. PlumbBob came up about four that afternoon and I headed back to check on the turkey. As I walked in the door everyone said PlumbBob was coming back in a hurry. Obviously he had seen the bear. Greg got ready to go.

PlumbBob arrived and told us the bear was coming directly to us, so he, Greg, Rob and I trotted to the runway. The bear was already near the lower end of the eleven hundred foot strip. The wind had gone calm or we would have been upwind of the bear. We hunkered down in a small copse of willows until at about eighty yards, Greg fired. The blond bear spun around trying to bite the spot of the bullet impact. Greg fired two more shots and the bear's struggles ceased.

This twelve year old boar showed the light colored collar which is usually not apparent in grizzlies past the age of three or four years. In grizzlies, a blond body with chocolate legs is referred to as "Toklat" coloration.

Greg's grizzly was shot on my deeded eighty acres, so we just drove the Honda to it, loaded it in the trailer and drove home to the lodge. After skinning we hung the hams alongside the caribou meat, anticipating a fine roast with rich gravy.

We wolfed down most of that big turkey, eating "like savages and kings" - who, I assume, eat whatever and however they please. All went to bed well fed and adequately lubricated to slip right into their sacks.

The next morning I was up to make coffee and by golly - the meat pole had been hit hard! Most of the quarters were missing and the frame had been drug about twelve yards south into the cranberry bog. We still had a cabin bear to deal with!

Careful inspection revealed one good paw print in a fresh pile of bear poop. This was a larger bear than the one we had just taken.

I told everyone to be certain to take their rifle to the outhouse, or they could take a 30/30 carbine that hung near the door. The carbine was safer to use than the pump shotgun. Everybody knows how to use the John Wayne western rifle.

Rob and I rebuilt the meat pole - an "A" frame - and rehung what we could recover of the caribou meat. The bear hams were gone, likely consumed.

PlumbBob was an Alaskan resident and needed no permit, so he said he would like to take the cabin bear. In the meantime, that afternoon Rob

PlumbBob and the evasive bull.

took him up into West Bowl canyon in mixed rain and snow, in pursuit of a caribou, which they harvested after two hours of climbing.

With all the excitement, the Kodiak boys had consumed most of their booze. I used the satellite phone to call my wife, Teresa. She was to purchase enough (a case) Jack Daniels for PlumbBob, Canadian Club for Grant and Smirnoff Vodka for Barry. She had never before been inside a liquor store. Then she was to take the cases of booze to Alaska Airlines, send it Gold Streak to Kotzebue, from there it would be chartered to the lodge. It was going to be pretty spendy booze.

Once the meat pole was up and hung, I ran a light cord from the nearest piece of meat to the willows closest to the lodge, then through the window. I tied a small bell to the cabin side of the cord. This should announce the return of the cabin bear.

Dinner was a fine variety of meat from caribou, domestic turkey and more caribou. Everyone was a bit on edge thinking about the problematic cabin grizzly that probably was lying nearby, possibly watching for a chance to wreak malicious mayhem on any of us he could touch. As Grant headed for the outhouse I reminded him to carry a firearm, to which he agreed.

After ten minutes or so we heard an awful scream from the direction of the outhouse. It did not sound human, it was more like a demonic cat. Barry said he knew the sound of a cougar. I turned off the Coleman lanterns and we all watched from the windows. Then it came to me that we should go check on Grant.

ALASKA CARIBOU

Our breath was condensing on the double pane windows when we heard the scream again. It was a frightening, chilling noise.

Then Barry noticed Grant coming from the outhouse and told us, he was familiar with the sound. It was Grant cleaning his hemorrhoids.

We all gave up on the bear about midnight and did not hear the bell that night. Morning light confirmed that the meat pole had not been touched.

We still had hunting to do and animals to tag. Greg and I walked north and just at the mouth of Break Ankle Creek, about a quarter of a mile from the lodge we found a band of resting caribou. Amongst the cluster of bodies rose a high, well balanced rack with long top tines. This was an impressive caribou to accompany his dandy bear.

We remained lying prone on the tundra for more than thirty minutes before the big bull gave Greg a clear shot. That was opportunity enough for my friend and the bull hit the ground with a broken neck. The rest of the mob of tundra deer jumped to their feet and charged our way, passing within twenty yards of where we were lying.

This was another easy pack of the meat and trophy to the lodge. Being a taxidermist, Greg caped this bull for a shoulder mount.

Greg's bull placed number three in the 2003 annual statewide competition.

Rob was coming up the creek with Barry and Grant, loaded down with caribou, so they had scored, too.

The emergency booze shipment, Gold Streaked from Kodiak came in on a chartered Cessna 185 that afternoon. The pilot left the cases near my cub, close to the runway.

So closed another active, successful day. We fed up, drank up and headed for bed. PlumbBob remained on one of the upstairs couches. Just after I put out the second Coleman lantern, the bell began to tinkle. PlumbBob slid open the side window and just below, standing next to the Honda three- wheeler, was a huge grizzly. PlumbBob leaned out the window and at a range of perhaps six yards - or less, he shot the bear. He stumbled toward the stairs, but I stopped him.

"I hit him, now we've got to go finish him off," PlumbBob blurted.

"Not in the dark, we're not," I said. "We'll get him in the morning."

We had a thick overcast with no moon with light snow falling. This called for another round of drinks. Before our guests were finished with talking over the day, I was back in my bunk.

A mist-like snow was still falling as the morning light reached the valley. In the reduced visibility I could make out the bulk of something out of place just beyond the three wheeler. As things got brighter the object became the carcass of a huge grizzly. It had taken only one or two steps after PlumbBob's bullet hit it. And it was a huge one!

When Greg saw the bear he said "I know that face. It's the one that mauled me three years ago!"

When Greg and I skinned the critter, its pelvis showed bone loss from an old wound and it had been dragging its non-functional left front leg. Greg reported hitting it twice as it came down the hill for

Grant and PlumbBob with the cabin grizzly. It took #3 in the statewide competition.

him. His first shot was high - the pelvic wound - and his second shot was point blank into the chest, which actually was a bit to the right of center, disabling the left front leg. We could not find a spent bullet, but the wounds verified Greg's claim.

The old boar was aged at twenty-three years by the Alaska Department of Fish and Game. It was not very fat and its teeth were not in good shape. Biologists told me that considering the poor body fat and the serious nature of the wounds, especially the front leg being disabled, the old bear may not have hibernated for the past two winters.

It's not likely that this is the same big grizzly that greeted Ron and the kids when they landed, as both Ron and Spencer would have noted and mentioned the crippled left front leg.

The bear had lain on the frozen ground for about nine hours when we began to photograph and skin the carcass. It's stiffness made good photos impossible, so we got the best picture after the skin was removed.

A few days later as I took the new hunters north through the heavy willows less than a hundred yards from the lodge I found the remains of several caribou quarters with bits of hanging cord attached. It appeared that grizzly had been eating and resting very close to the lodge.

On September 9 I flew Greg to town with his trophies and some meat. We got the bear hide and skull sealed for transportation outside Alaska. It was well salted, so Greg would take it and his caribou with him to Wyoming.

The group had pretty good success caribou hunting

The next morning I met the South African guests, but there were only two, a man and his twelve year old son. The fellow for whom I had picked up a left-over grizzly tag had suffered a mild heart attack back in late July, but never told me, apparently expecting to come anyway. He told the others he would not come weeks before I purchased the tag for him. I was not happy to hear that news.

The two incoming guests went up in the chartered Cessna 206. Rob could take care of them until I got up with the cub. I met the three men from Kodiak, got them checked in at Alaska Airlines and returned to the lodge just before dark. A large low pressure area was moving in from the south.

Not wanting to run out of booze again, the trio had ordered more than they drank, but that was okay. Most guests do not bring nearly enough for themselves and now we had a reserve supply in camp.

Rob and I soon learned that the young man from South Africa really liked fudge brownies. He had never eaten them before. We had plenty of Pillsbury packages, so we baked a batch every day for him.

This pleasant father and son were from the Northern Transvaal, which was renamed Mpumalanga after apartheid, and is the north and easterly state of the Republic of South Africa. Snow was a rarity in that part of the world and the twelve year old was hoping to see some. The next day it snowed for fourteen hours, leaving a cover ten inches deep.

In between snow flurries on the following day, Rob spotted a wolverine about a quarter of a mile north of the lodge. We all hustled up, found the fresh tracks, but lost the animal in the dense riparian willows. Returning to the lodge we came upon a bull moose of about fifty-eight inches in spread. The rutty animal watched us a moment, then went his own way, looking for love.

Rob is a Chief in the U.S. Coast Guard and had a jet to catch on Sept. 13. Luckily the weather improved and I was able to get him to town, then return to the lodge before dark. I had seen about 400 caribou in small scattered bands between town and the lodge, but none were within ten miles.

More gloom, cold and snow greeted us the next morning. We took foam insulated seat pads and glassed from the eastern moguls, but saw only one medium sized grizzly about five miles away and two cow moose. The young fellow enjoyed some sliding on a plastic toboggan I brought for him from town. These people loved salmon so I brought some frozen chums. We had three meals of salmon in three days. They could not get enough of the tasty fish.

The young man's wish for snow had been answered in spades. We made some short forays to the eastern moguls to glass, but we were not seeing any caribou. About all that was going for us was plenty of food and lodge comforts.

So these good natured people who had come so far, shot nothing, but the breeze. When we got to town I gave them two sets of caribou antlers from meat animals I had taken several years earlier. It was small compensation, but they seemed pleased.

Due to adverse wether I remained in Kotzebue until September 23. I reflected on the season. We had taken thirteen big game animals, including 2 grizzly bears, one Dall ram and ten caribou.

We observed at least fourteen different Grizzlies on Trail Creek this season. All berry species were few in number and small in size. Unlike most of GMU23, Trail Creek showed evidence of having had a very dry summer.

We saw no calf moose on Trail Creek this year. For the second season in a row, we observed no wolves on Trail Creek. We did see one Wolverine on at least 2 separate occasions.

We observed Dall sheep nearly every day from the lodge & elsewhere throughout upper Trail Creek, until the snowfall on Sept. 9, after which we did not notice any Dall sheep. I believe sheep numbers & age/sex cohorts were stable on Trail Creek.

Willow ptarmigan were not as abundant in 2001 as the previous year and in 2002 we saw very few ptarmigan, this trend continued in 2003.

Lemmings & voles were few in number, but we did observe a family of Red Fox, probably the same family as we reported for 2000, 2001 and 2002.

Arctic Char or Dolly Varden seemed to be in their normal numbers on upper Trail Creek, as were Grayling.

We observed marsh hawks, short eared owls, northern shrike, robins, stellar's jay and other usual bird species on Trail Creek this season.

I caught the ferry out of Homer on September 28 and was glad to be home.

Chapter Ten

2004 A Great Season

"In a hunting trip the days of long monotony of getting to the hunting ground and the days of unrequited toil after it has been reached always far outnumber the red-letter days of success. But it is these times that test the hunter." Theodore Roosevelt, The WildernessHunter, 1893.

So, I had been warned, and with those thoughts in mind I begin this tale with a briefing of events that normally take place before the actual hunts begin.

In 2004, for the first season since 1994, the Alaska Department of Fish and Game and the National Park Service agreed to allow a limited number of non-residents to hunt Dall sheep in northwest Alaska. I made applications for several would-be hunters and two were drawn for a permit. One of the two was my Wyoming guide friend, Greg Fischer, who had been terribly mauled by a grizzly in 2000, but he returned in 2003 to take a beautiful blond grizzly and a dandy caribou. The other lucky permit winner was Rex from Florida, for whom this would be his third trip to Trail Creek.

In all, I had booked eight guests, which makes a good season for me. I never liked crowded, over booked camps and have never overbooked, but its good to have three booking periods with two or three guest hunters for each period. I needed to depart Kodiak about ten days earlier than in recent years. I hated to miss those days of great King salmon fishing! I caught the ferry to Homer on August 9 and was in Anchorage by noon the next day.

By the end of the day on August 11 the annual inspection on the cub was completed and I took and passed my Biannual Flight review and check ride the next day. It's a required and reasonable formality.

Smoke from wild fires made August 12 unsuitable for a VFR trip to Kotzebue, so I bought a new plexiglas windshield and installed it in the cub.

It cost only a hundred and eighty dollars and was easy to replace in just over an hour of work. The clear window seemed to improve the visibility conditions, but the smoke remained, so I visited the Tanana Valley State Fair.

Saturday, August 14 the smoke was worse. I did some shopping and shipped a hundred and ninety pounds of food to Kotzebue for a hundred and ten dollars. Forecast was for improvement so I topped the tanks off with fifty one gallons of hundred octane aviation fuel at three dollars and fifty cents per gallon. I ate at Taco Bell and went to bed feeling good.

Sunday the smoke was still bad in Fairbanks but incoming jets said the top was about four thousand feet, so I called the tower for a special clearance to depart and was airborne by 9:30. I climbed above the dense smoke and found good visibility just below five thousand feet. Winds aloft were good and I made most of the four hundred and forty miles to Kotzebue at nine thousand five hundred feet. I landed in Kotzebue in under five hours.

Things were pretty good, but for the freezer which I unplugged to let thaw and clean before I added my frozen food. Most renters are unthoughtful it seems.

The favorable easterly tail winds brought the interior smoke with me. I did some pre-season preparatory stuff in town before heading up to the lodge at 2:30pm. It was fifty-two degrees and calm. About half way the air got really thick and a mix of fog and smoke went all the way to the ground. I muddled my way through the foothills and got to the Noatak River, then found the mouth of the Kuguroruk River and followed it to Trail Creek. I saw a band of about a thousand caribou near Kayak Lake and animals were scattered all the way to the lodge. Four single bears were near the river just south of the lodge. I landed at 4:30. It was plus sixty-eight degrees, calm, and with no mosquitos at the home strip.

I offloaded the full load of food, gear and fuel and made a quick return to town.

The second story of the lodge had only one layer of 3/8 inch plywood on it and it was doing fine after twenty-four years, but I wanted to add another course of plywood. The local store had some plywood so I purchased twenty-six sheets of 5/8 inch, and split then down the middle. The two foot by eight foot pieces would fit easily into a Cessna 206 charter. I took the cut wood to Haagelands hanger to leave for the last trip to the lodge to pick up departing guests.

After filling one of my two gas trailers with four hundred gallons of hundred octane at $1,370, I parked the trailer at my tie down spot. As I was leaving, a pilot from Montana stopped by. He told me that he was taking his PA-12 Super Cruiser and going home rather than fly for a Transporter in Arctic conditions. Blue Bird weather is rare in northwestern Alaska, as are Blue Bird pilots.

Weather was five hundred feet overcast with south wind at thirty knots and one mile visibility when I took my grandson Spencer to the lodge - as always I had a big load of stuff for the soon to begin season. We found somewhat better ceilings and visibility sixty miles north of town and caribou were showing up in small scattered bands. I got Spencer in, started one Honda three wheeler and hauled the freight to the buildings, then headed back to town.

Greg Fischer, my guide friend from Wyoming came in on the early flight on Thursday. He had hunted with me in 2003 and took a beautiful blond boar grizzly and a caribou that was number three in the statewide competition. This season he was drawn for a Dall ram permit. This was to be the first non-subsistence Dall sheep hunt in northwest Alaska since 1994. I was confident we would have a good opportunity to take a ram.

The wild fire smoke that had delayed my departure from Fairbanks now covered most of the northern part of Alaska. One could smell and taste the smoke, it was so thick. Visibility was reduced to one mile or less. I got a special VFR clearance to take Greg to the lodge.

A north wind of about twenty miles per hour had come up and I hoped it would clear the smoke from the area, but improvement was slow. It took an hour and forty-five minutes flying to get Greg to camp and only an hour and fifteen minutes to return to Kotzebue.

Spencer reported good rams on Middle Mountain to the east and more in the West Bowl. Caribou were scattered throughout Trail Creek Valley. I told Spencer to try to kill a fat barren cow for an older lady friend, Beulah, and skin its legs appropriately for making mukluks. It would be good to also take two fat bulls for me to take to town on the next trip, as I had two guests to bring in and nothing to take out. There were plenty of people in town who would appreciate some fresh, fat meat. Greg could help with packing the meat, but I reminded Spencer to not allow Greg to carry too much as his leg was still bothering him after being so badly broken in the bear mauling four years earlier.

Kotzebue was still below VFR minimums, so I had to get a special clearance to land. I filled the main fuel tanks and met my new guests, an attorney and his wife at the NuLukVik Hotel. They were set to go the next morning, although they were a bit anxious about the smoke. Milton casually mentioned that his wife Mary was diabetic and needed her meds to be kept under refrigeration. It's good that he gave me that much notice. I put some empty plastic whiskey bottles in the freezer and gathered up ice cubes from friends to make up an adequate cold pack for the insulin.

My old friend and at one time, almost my uncle, Art Fields was sitting by his house so I took him some frozen halibut and visited. Art was reportedly the first Alaska Native from the Arctic to be licensed as a Registered Guide. He and I had done a lot together, in spite of him being twenty-five years my senior. In 1967 he took me out on the ice to observe polar bears. He was an unlicensed pilot then, now he had closed his flying career.

Two years before I purchased a Garmin 55 GPS which proved to be a great navigation device in bad weather and smoke. I took off with Mary, the hunter's wife, who expressed her concern about the thick smoke. We

Jake and Art Fields shooting the breeze at the Chucki seaside.

2004 A Great Season

climbed to nine thousand feet to get well over the highest peaks enroute. We could not see the ground, but I felt safe in letting down when we were forty miles south of the lodge. At about two thousand feet above ground level we could make out the course of the Kuguroruk River, so I followed that into the mountains where visibility improved. Mary was relieved to be on the ground and inside the lodge.

Spencer had two bulls and the cow cut up, clean, and ready to go to friends in town.

My return to Kotzebue was at high altitude due to the heavy smoke. I distributed the fat meat, and the skin for Beulah, fueled up and returned with the hunter, Milt at 4pm. This time I flew at one thousand feet along the western foothills of the Eli River. I resolved to buy a newer model GPS with a moving map.

Both mature bulls were in fine shape. Neck shots made for no meat loss.

Greg and Spencer had baked salmon and potatoes ready which we ate before sighting in Milt's rifle. We had a good visit until bedtime at 11pm.

Early the next morning, through the still present smoke, I spotted a very large grizzly feeding on the alluvial fan across the creek. The thick smoke and poor visibility encouraged us to hang around the lodge.

On Sunday the smoke cleared by mid-morning, so Greg and I headed for the West Bowl to get a closer look a the big ram Spencer had reported.

We scaled the gravel ridge to Salz Point then continued into the deep canyon. The last time I had walked this path was nineteen years before with our lone Alaskan U.S. Congressman, Don Young. After passing through one broad cleft we stopped on the ridge line to glass. Below, I spotted what appeared to be a bone, bleached white and huge. I asked Greg what it looked like to him and he agreed with my call - it was a large femur.

It was at least four feet long and heavy. It may have been from a wooly mammoth, but I had never before seen mammoth remains in such a spot, so high in the mountains. Most of the prehistoric animal bones are found in thawing permafrost banks or along streams.

We continued further, deeper into the drainage. When we came to an especially difficult rocky outcrop, Greg said he wasn't up to that. His leg was bothering and his balance was not up to par. So we turned back. I planned to descend to the large bone, but before we reached it, I looked back and saw the big ram lying with its back to us. A quick check with binoculars confirmed it was the one we were after. We were above and had been exposed to it for at least five minutes, but it was looking away from us, into the canyon. That's very unusual.

The ram stood up and began walking away, never looking at us. At two hundred yards, Greg missed the first shot, but connected with the second. The ram bunched up, then fell over backward and rolled down the hill for fifty yards. When we reached the ram, we noticed the right eye was opaque, indicating blindness. That's why it hadn't seen us and spooked.

Wild sheep normally have very large testicles, but the right one on this ram was several times larger than the left, and far larger than any I had seen in the more than one hundred rams I had helped guests collect in the past thirty-seven years. The ram was fat and healthy in appearance. I removed the scrotum with both testicles for delivery to the local biologist.

Greg and the half-blind ram, the first sport killed ram in ten years.

Due to Greg's compromised leg, I packed out the meat and he brought the head and cape. It was seven thirty in the evening when we started back to the lodge. At ten o'clock we reached the west moguls above Trail Creek.

From our resting spot I noticed Spencer and Milt sneaking up a gut in the alluvial fan and coming our way. Then I saw what had brought them. A dandy lone caribou bull was lying about four hundred yards below us

2004 A Great Season

and an equal distance from the hunters. Greg and I just sat and watched the stalk. In a few minutes Spencer told Milt to shoot and the caribou just rolled over in its bed.

Greg and I headed for the lodge, leaving Spencer to gut out the animal and leave most of the meat until tomorrow when I would return with him.

We got to the lodge footsore at midnight, hung the sheep meat, had a quick snack of canned stew along with a whiskey and hit the sack.

The large bodied bull had great main bean length which pleased the Milt.

Seems to me that everyone sleeps well after a physically taxing day like we'd had. That coupled with no mechanical noises, and lulled by the faint burbling of the nearby Dipwater Creek, makes for restful slumber.

Sheep tenderloins and heart went well with pancakes, after which Spencer, Milt and I returned to Milt's caribou. We made short work of caping, loading and packing the meat.

After replacing an elbow and a two foot section of chimney pipe on the sauna stove, I placed four square sided old gas cans full of water on the stove to heat for bathing that evening.

Greg set up the outside fire pit to cook the ribs and potatoes for dinner. It was just another day in paradise.

Tuesday was clear with visibility unlimited and a light northerly breeze. Milt had purchased tickets for himself and wife to visit Mount McKinley if time permitted. He had his critter, so he asked to be taken to town. I took a load of meat in, arranged for the Cessna 206 charter to haul as much of the cut plywood as possible on the trip to pick up the departing guests. The couple was in town before six o'clock pm, so after getting the antlers boxed and checked in, they invited me to join them for dinner at the hotel.

Things had gone perfectly. This couple were in and out in five days with a fine trophy.

Milt and his wife took me to breakfast at the local eatery, the old Golden Whale, now called the Bayside. After their jet took off I went to my nephew,

Kenny Ubben's shop to work on a replacement wheel for the wheel borrow at camp.

After nine o'clock I took the abnormal sheep scrotum to the National Park Service office which was supervised by a new lady. When I showed her the scrotum she was controlled, but upset, as she told me to "take that thing out of her office."

Surprised at her reaction I suggested that she call the NPS chief sheep biologist in Fairbanks. She motioned me out of the office as she dialed. I was standing on the porch - holding the bag, so to speak - when she called me back to take the phone. I brought the scrotum in hand and took the phone in my free hand. The biologist thanked me and told me he chewed the lady out and told her to never treat a cooperator like that. The supervisor called in another employee and instructed her to put the scrotum in the refrigerator until the biologist could take it. He was coming the next day.

Later that year the sheep biologist told me that the testicles I turned in showed the ram had brucellosis. This was the first and only case of that disease in Alaskan wild sheep. He thanked me again for bringing in the scrotum. I believe that to this day in 2021, there have been no other reported cases of brucellosis in Dall sheep. Thank goodness for that!

A few years earlier a friend of mine from Kotzebue was diagnosed as having contracted brucellosis. It was believed that he contracted it from an infected caribou. He recovered without complications.

Brucellosis is an infectious disease caused by bacteria called Brucella. Many different animal species and humans can become ill. I read that Brucellosis is primarily a reproductive disease in animals, but it can also cause reoccurring fevers, arthritis or udder infection (mastitis).

On my trip back to Trail Creek I encountered thirty knot headwinds from ground level to nine thousand feel. When I landed at Trail Creek downdrafts were strong so I landed straight in on the six hundred foot cross wind strip and used less than two hundred feet to stop. It was plus twenty-four degrees at altitude and my aircraft cabin heat was not working.

The Western Arctic Caribou Herd, which roams the areas I hunt had reached the highest population known, which was estimated to be six hundred thousand animals. Even from high altitude I saw thousands of caribou from thirty miles north of Kotzebue all the way to the lodge.

2004 A Great Season

Thursday morning was clear and plus thirty-eight degrees with about fifteen knots of north wind. Greg, Spencer and I walked south, thinking of fishing. Near the end of the runway we noticed a young caribou running our way. It was followed by two grey wolves which appeared to be an adult and a pup of the year. The boys had no shooting opportunity on the wolves, but later Spencer shot two big bull caribou and a lone cow with the largest rack I have ever seen on a cow. She was barren - a prime meat animal. With so many caribou, there was no reason not to take as many as possible to give to friends and family for meat.

As my companions hung the meat and got supper, I worked on the heater on the cub. A cable had slipped. It was an easy repair.

Sometimes the wind seems to get tired and the next day it was light and variable. Overnight temperature had dropped to plus twenty degrees. My friends Warren and Mae Thompson landed and reported that the only place they had seen caribou was on Trail Creek. I was happy to give them one of the two bulls we had hanging.

Ravens frequented the roof of the lodge, especially in winter. They peck the tar paper to get gravel. I brought up a fiberglas owl which we mounted on the peak of the roof. It held the ravens at bay for a few days, before one bold bird pooped on it. So much for deterrence!

Saturday, Greg's day of departure came too soon. Again it was clear with unlimited visibility and sub-freezing temperature. Dozens of caribou were in all quadrants, feeding and resting. We got Greg's gear loaded and saw a capital bull across the creek. I encourage my friend to shoot it. With some reluctance he did take it. It scored 405 points and in November, 2005 we learned that it placed number two in the annual statewide competition.

This bull had only five top points on each side, but its bez and shovels were very good. The rack was symmetrical and pleasing in conformation. It was a large, robust animal with plenty of fat.

Spencer and Greg with the fine last minute bull.

We flew to town at six thousand feet with a generous tail wind, landing after only one and a quarter hours in the air.

Word in town was that one of the high volume and otherwise notorious Transporters had lost a DeHaviland Otter enroute from Anchorage to Kotzebue with pilot and guests aboard. In bad smoke conditions the aircraft had become separated from another plane owned by the same company. A search had been called, but was hampered by adverse visibility. The Civil Air Patrol was calling for volunteers to join the search. The company's second airplane did not join the search, instead it set about putting out hunters in the Noatak area. That was disgusting, in my view.

Spencer and Greg with the fine last minute bull.

After refueling and getting Greg ready for an early morning departure, we picked up Art Fields and all had a burger at a little joint next to Art's house. We took some caribou meat to LaVonne's bed and breakfast five miles down the beach and enjoyed a glass of wine with her.

My three guests from Florida, Rex on his third trip with me, David and Larry were delayed until the late flight so they stayed in the Nu Luk Vik Hotel. Many called it the No Luck Hotel, but it was nice by Arctic standards.

Rex and Larry, along with my Assistant, Mike, went up in the Cessna 206 charter. David remained, at his request, to fly with me in the cub. Spencer came out on the charter to report back to his day job.

David and I arrived a bit after four that afternoon. He was impressed with all the game we saw - thousands of caribou, many Dall sheep, six grizzlies and four large bull moose.

Supper was local King crab - smaller than that of Kodiak, but perhaps the sweetest of all King crab, baked salmon, corn and chocolate cake.

I changed the oil in the cub, keeping the waste oil for use in the sauna stove. We were all in bed by eleven pm as rain and fog filled the valley.

On August 31, morning came at six with plus forty-six degrees, south wind at eight knots and visibility of a quarter mile in rain, mist and fog. My gauge showed an inch and a half of rain fell in the night.

After pancakes by Larry we got after some caribou on the northwest alleuvlal fan. David downed a mature bull and we had it back across the rapidly rising river by mid afternoon.

Wednesday, September first, marked the opening of grizzly season. David had the only permit. We glassed the fresh caribou gut pile but found only ravens. The fog lifted by mid morning. There were sheep showing everywhere we looked, from Middle Mountain to the South Overlook and all along the western side of the valley. We counted forty-six sheep from the lodge windows, of which eighteen were rams.

A smiling David with the first caribou for his group.

Rex had a sheep permit and liked the looks of a ram on Middle Mountain, so off he, Mike and I went. It was a straight shot up the middle spine of the mountain. Mike had reservations about the steepness. I talked with him a little on that, then we kept climbing.

Animals in the valley are seldom hunted and therefore not accustomed to people. Sheep had not been hunted here for ten years. The stalk was simple and put us directly above the ram. Rex shot at less than one hundred yards and the big ram tumbled down the slope.

The beautiful ram showed signs of rutting battles, but neither horn was broomed.

Rex with his well more than full curl ram.

This ram was a taker for anyone, but we would not learn of just how well it compared with other sheep taken in Alaska in 2004 until December, 2005, when we learned it scored number one in the Alaskas Statewide competition.

With departure about eleven in the morning and return by eleven that night, it had been a full, and thoroughly satisfying day.

We all awoke, well rested and happy to see a high overcast and little wind. Sheep rested unconcerned on both sides of the valley while caribou strolled about like weekend shoppers in a mall. It looked like multiple opportunities on the hoof for my guests. We needed to be very selective in choosing which animals to pursue from such a huge selection. We decided to walk toward the South Overlook as that area had not been visited for two weeks. David had a grizzly permit to fill and I was hoping to encounter wolves.

By noon we had looked at more than five hundred caribou, of which perhaps ten percent were mature bulls. In the dwarf birch just north of the esker we call "Indian Point" was a lone bull that Larry wanted to take back home with him. With minimal cover between that animal and us, I left Mike, David and Rex on the hillside with instructions to pursue any animal they found desirable while Larry and I focused on his selected bull.

We went slowly, at times crawling over slight rises in the brushy lowland fan, as we narrowed the shooting distance to about two hundred and fifty yards. I filmed with my video camera as Larry carefully squeezed off his shot. The caribou did not flinch. Another shot and the bull turned to look at us. I told Larry he was shooting over the animal, so he should hold for the bottom of the brisket just aft of the front legs. On the third shot the big bull went down as if brain-shot. His bullet had struck the animal three inches from the base of the skull. No meat loss with this one.

Larry's rifle was shooting high and a bit to the right. We corrected that at the shooting range with a soft rest.

As usual I caped the animal, then gutted it. I went forward two ribs from the last and cut the carcass in two pieces. Mike volunteered to carry the front half, so I tied the hind half on my board. Larry insisted on carrying out the head and cape. It was an easy pack to the meat rack. An animal per day sets a nice pace for any hunt. I set the frozen turkey in the kitchen to cook the next afternoon.

A nice bull, medium in body size, but carrying a dandy set of headgear.

September third opened with plus thirty degrees, a thin layer of ice on the edges of dip water creek and a light skiff of snow covering everything.

Punctuating the snow on the west fan were about one hundred and fifty caribou. Not to be outdone, the east fan hosted a similar number of feeding animals. Just off the end of the main runway Rex saw a bull he wanted to take, so he and I grabbed our rifles and hustled down through the marginal willows to within easy shooting range. He shot dropped the caribou. We reached the animal and I asked Rex for his metal locking tag, but he had forgotten it at the lodge. State law requires that the hunter carry his license, permits and tags at all times and that any animal be tagged immediately. Along came Larry and David, as Rex returned for his tag.

Of course just then, as Murphy's Law would have it, for the first time since 911, a helicopter came rapidly up the valley. It was a charter 'copter from Fairbanks and carried a National Park Service Ranger and an Alaska

State Protection Officer - game wardens. I sent Larry to tell Rex to hurry with the tag, while I walked to the helicopter and engaged the officials in conversation. I was confident that no problem would arise and the issue of the tag never came up. That was just as well.

Our visit was pleasant and I invited the pilot and his two passengers to come to the lodge for a coffee. The caribou got tagged. At my insistence the officials looked over my paperwork and judged it in order before flying on to check another guide operation. The state officer commented on the number of my Master Guide license - #54. It was the lowest number he had seen. They spent a pleasurable hour with us.

Not long after the chopper departed, in came an Alaska Department of Fish and Game super cub flown by the local Protection Officer. This, too, led to a pleasant conversation and a cup of coffee that lasted about an hour. This game cop said he wished everyone would bring out their caribou in two pieces, as we had. The turkey was smelling delicious so I invited the State game cop to join us, but he had to travel on to other camps to check.

So we were checked by a total of three game wardens in one afternoon. Makes a person wonder. But nothing was amiss.

Mike had finished fleshing the sheep and one caribou cape, so we salted them both. The ram's horns measured thirty-seven and 7/8 inches in length -which is long for a Brooks Range sheep. I aged it at twelve and a half years.

Our three guests, Mike and I gorged on turkey, potatoes and gravy and fresh baked brownies.

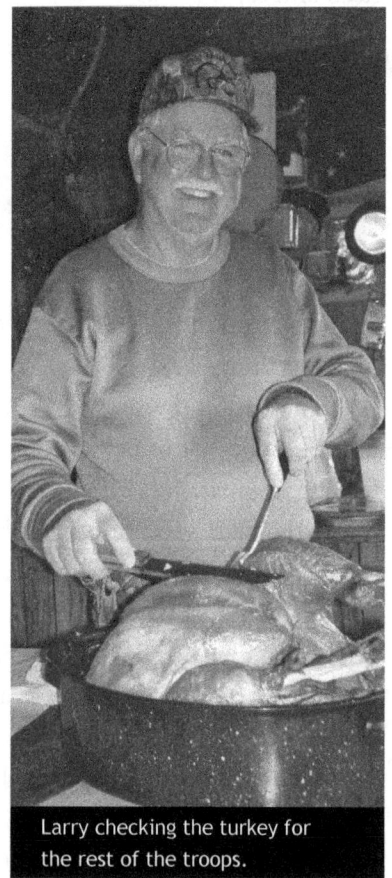
Larry checking the turkey for the rest of the troops.

On Sunday I took Rex to Kotzebue for him to call home regarding Hurricane Frances. He was in farming and was especially worried about his citrus orchards. The flight was beautiful. I took in his sheep horns and cape and two sets of caribou horns and capes, along with choice cuts of meat. Everything was fine at Rex's business and home. We returned with a new forty pound bottle of propane and a few fresh vegetables. I flew back at six thousand, five hundred feet and even at that altitude, we had caribou in sight the entire trip.

Larry had dinner ready when we landed. It was barbecued caribou ribs, baked potatoes and green salad with a new batch of brownies. Most of our groups of guests are pleasant, but this bunch was especially delightful.

David was after a grizzly so I took him to the South Overlook early the next day. We saw hundreds of caribou and two bull moose, but no bears. My left outboard ankle bone became painful on our return. When I took my boot and sock off, it looked nasty.

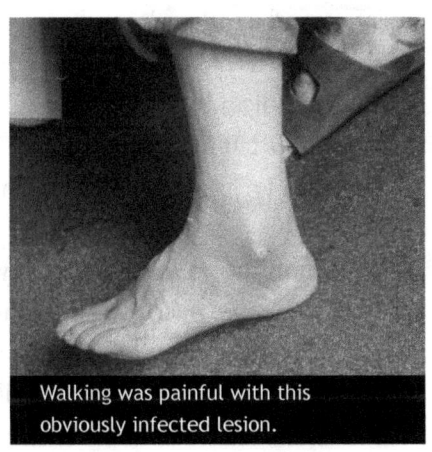

Walking was painful with this obviously infected lesion.

I had no idea what had caused the swollen lesion, but it was "pointing," so I had Larry lance it with a skin (Glovers) needle. It drained some pus, and that relieved it some. I swallowed a Zithromax antibiotic and soaked my ankle it in salt water before going to bed.

The next morning the ankle looked better but was still plenty sore. I took another Zithromax. I sent the three hunters with Mike back to the south while I cleaned up the lodge and kept glassing out the windows. Thirty minutes after they left I found a large grizzly grazing in a blue berry patch just across Break Ankle Creek, a quarter of a mile north of the lodge, so I put a flag up to signal Mike to return.

Mike saw the flag and came back. I took David to the still feeding bear. The large bear was going after blue berries like a kid in a candy shop. It seemed to be in a form of sheer bruin ecstasy.

We crossed the creek and climbed the five foot bank to within a hundred yards of the target. I reminded my guest to aim for the middle of the shoulder and then reload and keep shooting until the bear was down. David smacked the bear in the left shoulder. The bear took off like a track runner off the blocks and David hit it again with two more shots. The next shot caused the bear to turn around and bite the afflicted area, the third shot dropped it.

David and the bear he waited for. The lodge is just over his left shoulder.

This grizzly had an especially nice looking face. Some are rather ugly, but not this one. It was a boar that showed no scars or signs of being in serious fights with other bears. It had a twenty-four inch skull and the hide squared seven feet six inches. This animal had a tattoo in its left axilla that read "1707." Its estimated age was twelve to fifteen years. I never did get the information on this animal from the Depart of Fish and Game.

With nothing pressing, I took my time skinning this animal closely to avoid having to go over it again in the little time remaining for this group. It smelled good, so as I do with most bears, I brought in the hams.

A cool mist descended on the valley as we got to the lodge. Across the creek were several dozen bull caribou, so we went to take a closer look, but found nothing that David wanted to shoot.

The other group had gone to the South Overlook where they saw caribou and large flocks of ptarmigan, but they shot nothing. When they arrived I had a large pot of spaghetti ready. My left ankle was doing fine, but I stayed on Zithromax for five days.

In the morning, after pancakes, Mike took Rex and Larry south again, while I removed the paws from the bear hide. David cleaned the skull. We were completed before noon, so we walked up to the east moguls to glass. Just below us came a band of eighty or ninety caribou, which included a bull with the best rack I had seen that season. I encouraged David to shoot it as he had originally planned to take two and had an unused tag. After a little contemplation David said he would leave it for his friends. I told him it was doubtful they would get a chance to even see it, let alone take it, but he would not shoot. I was disappointed.

Rex, Larry and Mike drug in a bit before dark. They had spooked the band of caribou with the outstanding bull, never seeing the big one when the animals ran into East Bowl valley. I figured we'd never see any of those animals again.

After the meal of caribou backstraps, corn and salad I glanced out the window as I was doing dishes to see the outstanding bull in a large group of animals on the runway!

After convincing Rex that he should take that bull we easily walked down the trail to the runway and when the big bull was clear of the others, Rex shot him. The animal reared up and hobbled around with one leg disabled, then dropped to the ground near a runway marker. The mob of caribou deserted the wounded one just as it fell to the ground.

Rex had taken several caribou with me since his first hunt in 1996 and received the second place "Big Three" award in 1998, but this bull was clearly the best he had taken. It scored over four hundred points and earned first place in the 2004 statewide competition.

Rex with his second caribou of the trip.

Larry was still looking for another caribou or a big moose, so I sent him and Mike to the high part of the East Moguls. Rex and David had all the game they wanted, so they walked north to make some photos. I cleaned up the kitchen, then got things ready to take to town with Rex. I tied two sets of caribou antlers on the wing struts, loaded Rex's stuff and we took off for Kotzebue at four o'clock.

Out flight was delightful with a high overcast and no turbulence. We were insight of caribou for most of the trip.

After securing the meat and checking Rex in at the hotel I called my friend Wayne Anthony Ross (WAR). He and Jim Land, secretary of the National Rifle Association, would not arrive until September 15. Worse yet, they would have only three days to hunt. Major Jim Land trained Carlos Hathcock, the famous Marine sniper from Viet Nam, and helped set up the Marine sniper school. I was looking forward to meeting him.

The Cessna charter arrived with Mike and two guests at eleven, but did not bring all the meat, so I would need to go up to get the last load. A blizzard was forecast, so I needed to get up and back as soon as possible. The last of my load of split plywood siding was stacked on the runway. I had loaded the cub with lumber and other materials which I left with the large pile on the runway. I picked up the meat, covered and weighted down the siding, locked up the Honda and the buildings and was back in town by seven.

So I had four full days before the Wayne and Jim were due. It was Saturday, so I attended the high school track run to watch some of my grand kids. That afternoon I distributed caribou meat to eight families.

On Monday, September 13 I took a load of lumber and some stove oil to the lodge. I landed at five that evening. It was plus twenty degrees with light wind and a little snow on the runway. I used the Honda and trailer to take the last of the split plywood to storage in the little original building.

I always tried to fill the cub with useful stuff rather than go up empty.

Just before dark a huge herd of caribou came streaming down from the north. A superb bull, one of the three best I had seen in 37 years, stood just feet from the meat rack, but I could not shoot the same day airborne. I wished I had come the day before. I figured about sixty-five hundred animals passed close to the lodge in the last hour of daylight.

At eight o'clock the next morning it was plus twenty degrees with a north wind of thirty knots. There were thousands of caribou on both sides of the valley. I had a cup of coffee, as I searched with binoculars for the fine bull of the evening before, but I did not find him. I shot three mature bulls for meat and took them directly to the cub. After closing up the buildings I headed to town.

From the lodge window. Part of a long string of southward moving caribou.

Wayne Ross and Jim Land arrived on the noon jet the next day. Many hunters in camouflage came in to be dropped off by Transporters. It seemed that everyone recognized Jim Land. Luckily their gear arrived with them. I dropped Jim at my daughter Sandy's house, then took WAR north. When I picked up Jim, I bought a pie and grabbed some local King crab that Mike had given me. We landed at nine, just before dark. It was plus twenty-five degrees with a gusty twenty knot north wind. There were still hundreds of caribou in the valley.

We ate some fried caribou, canned corn and pie as we sipped on WAR's Jack Daniels whiskey. It was midnight before we quit talking.

In the morning Jim asked if I had a shooting range.

"Why yes, Major Land, I have a five hundred meter range for you, Sir," I replied.

"Well, set 'er up," he said.

I put an old five gallon gas can about five hundred yards from the end of the runway. Shooting offhand, Major Land hit it with all three shots. At age 69 he and had not lost his edge on shooting.

Conditions remained the same as we walked north to look over caribou on the fan south of Current Creek. We found no big bulls so we let the penetrating wind and flurries of snow push us back to the lodge. Supper was Arctic King crab, garlic bread, pie and whiskey. We saw brilliant, active Northern Lights that clear, cold night.

On the seventeenth we saw very few caribou. The cold wind was still strong out of the north and it looked like the critters had gone south on us.

This was scheduled to be the next to last day at camp. The number of animals coming down the creek had slowed to an intermittent dribble, so in the afternoon we decided that a young bull was better than nothing. It would taste just fine on the table.

WAR and Jim Land. Where there had been thousands, now there were few.

The vole population was not high this year, but on a couple of occasions, at dusk we were entertained by several short eared owls gliding over the cranberry bog just east of the lodge, occasionally dropping to seize a vole. The robins had departed, but a pair of Northern Shrikes hunted near the buildings, often hovering near the window as they looked us over.

A good meal of caribou, spuds, salad and fresh baked brownies, followed by cigars and fine whiskey made it a memorable evening.

On Sunday, the nineteenth I took Jim Land to town. It was plus eighteen degrees with light wind, making the trip pleasant, if a bit chilly in the cub. I took Jim to the sod house, or shack actually, that I use when in

Kotzebue. I loaded up some dunnage lumber and fuel oil and went back for WAR.

Closing the lodge for winter takes less than an hour. I ran the Honda out of gas, turned off the propane, shuttered the windows and locked up. WAR and I were in Kotzebue by eight that evening. WAR ordered a pizza for dinner and we visited until midnight.

The next day the Alaska Airlines flight was delayed from noon until nine that evening, so I gave my guests a tour of Kotzebue.

My ferry trip from Homer to Kodiak was rescheduled for September 30. I prefer to spend time at the lodge rather than elsewhere, so I went back up. It would have been so much better with one of my Labradors. either Max or Zeke. I do miss them.

One well placed shot to the neck anchored the young bull.

As I landed I saw five large wolves on the cutback near the end of the runway. Just before dark I glassed a huge grizzly scuffling around the spot of one of my caribou kills of the previous week. Larry, Jim or WAR would have been happy to have it. I had seen this big boar for several years, always in late September, but never put anyone in position to shoot it. I had a few minor things to do, so I only spent two nights before heading south. The creeks were icing up and the country was changing from technicolor to a black and white world. Things happen rapidly as full winter sets in, the bears go to bed and everything else seems to slow down. The Technicolor world fades to dull gray.

Two days in Kotzebue were spent leisurely as I waited for favorable conditions to fly to Fairbanks. I waited for what appeared to be a safe hole in between two large storm systems, but I encountered greater than forecast winds, turbulence and clouds. Comparison of my airspeed with the GPS ground speed indicated the winds at my different altitudes were in excess of fifty miles per hour in some places. I got through without having to land until I got to Chena Marina.

A friend saw me fly over and drove to greet me at the dirt field. He expressed surprise at my arrival, given the conditions, and offered me a shot of whiskey. I took a sip and told him I would not knowingly make the decision to fly in such conditions, as I had the most valuable cargo aboard that I had ever carried.

"Gold, Jake?" he asked.

"Nope, I've got my kids Dad aboard," was my reply.

With over one hundred pounds of prime caribou for friends in Fairbanks and Anchorage, my load was heavy. In all I gave significant portions of meat to more than a dozen individuals and families in the fall of 2004. Then, with transporting deer hunters at Kodiak, I distributed another thousand pounds or more of venison.

The ferry *M/V KENNECOTT* docked in Kodiak at eight in the morning of October 1. Teresa and the girls met me, anxious to see what surprises I might have from the big town. I always tried to bring some exotic treats, such as olives of different types and preparations, cheeses, exotic fruits and other things not available in Kodiak.

At different times our daughters had several types of pets, or domestic stock animals, over the years. They had parakeets that nested and raised chicks in our living room, hamsters, a Surinam Toad, domestic rabbits, and one year we raised a pair of hogs. For a summer and fall they tended a wet nanny goat and her kid. The girls learned to milk and use goat milk instead of cow's squeezings. We had five little red hens that produced brown eggs. The kids loved gathering the eggs, but they were not so keen on cleaning the poop covered things. But they did it.

This year, feeling somewhat pressed to find something really unique, I found some carnivorous plants at Home Depot in Anchorage. The Venus Fly Trap, Pitcher Plant and Sundew Plant were initially fascinating to the girls, ages nine and ten, but they were not quite what my daughters were expecting. The meat eating vegetables were not cuddly. Bess and Kate soon grew tired of catching flies to feed their new pets.

2004 A Great Season

A nice gathering of home grown brown eggs.

My wife and I always emphasized being practical in one's activities to the girls. The girls told me they thought the chickens were much more useful to us than the carnivorous plants. I had to agree.

It had not been a perfect year, but it certainly wasn't a bad one us and our guests. We harvested seventeen big game animals at Trail Creek. including two Dall sheep, fourteen caribou and one grizzly bear.

Perhaps our greatest harvest was the collection of fine memories the time had provided.

Chapter Eleven
2005 Another Exceptional Year

So many unforeseen events took place this year. On May 7, I received a call from my daughter Sandy's friend, Daisy, that Sandy had fallen ill and was to be medevaced to Anchorage. They feared she had a stroke. She was only 47 years old. We heard no more until the next day when the CatScan showed a massive brain tumor, that was judged to be operable. Sandy asked me to come to Anchorage to be with her kids.

On May 11, Sandy was in surgery for five hours, the doctor, a specialist flown in from New York City assured me the tumor was benign and she would recover with one hundred percent of her mental and physical faculties. That evening the hospital allowed the first visitors. Sandy asked for me, her daughter Scarlett, and her son Seth.

Before we entered her room I told the kids that they should tell their Mom how beautiful she is and not to show alarm at her shaved head. When we walked in, Sandy was smiling and I blurted out "Nice eyebrows, Sandy!" Everyone, most of all Sandy, got a hearty laugh. Family and friends visited the chapel and offered our thanks to God for this best possible outcome of a frightening situation.

The news reported that some student pilot flew a Cessna 140 too close to the White House resulting in two jets being scrambled and full terrorism alarms.

On Thursday, May 12, I picked up my son, Martin and his wife to stay with Sandy and I went home to Kodiak on the late flight.

My commercial fishing and big game Transporting partner, Tom Dooley, had his seiner, the *M/V REBEL* in Seattle being rebuilt after an engine room fire the previous July. Repairs were delayed. Originally the boat was to be ready to sail in March. After much persuasion, I had convinced my wife to allow our daughters, Bess and Kate, to accompany me to help Tom bring the boat back to Kodiak. We planned to stop on the way in most of the towns in southeast Alaska. It would be a great adventure for the kids. But the repair job was delayed, which kept the girls from making the trip.

The deadline for submission of grizzly and sheep drawing permits was May 31, so I needed to be close to home for last minute applicants, but Tom needed the boat back in Kodiak as soon as possible to allow him to outfit and go to Bristol Bay for salmon tendering. All the people who had asked to make the trip, backed out. I could not live with myself if he made the trip alone and had serious problems, so I told him I would come down on May 22. I was not looking forward to the trip at this critical time, but I felt I had to do it.

When I arrived, the boat yard was operating very inefficiently. Most of the workers did not speak English, many were from Poland and Latvia and were poorly supervised. Tom and I worked long hours until we were at last able to depart on May 25. We passed through the Ballard

Jake and Fred when the boat was finally ready.

Locks allowing us to leave Lake Union and enter Elliott Bay. Each of us put on a survival suit, to make sure we could and the suits were functional - just in case. As we were in the locks I called home to learn that my good friend from Germany, Ulrich, had a hunter who wanted a grizzly permit, so with the help of my sister, the application was made on time. Unfortunately, due to my absence, two other last minute applications were not made. So we would have only one bear hunter for the fall season.

My old friend, Fred Muhs, a lumberman/rancher from Idaho joined us, so we would have an extra man to watch the wheel during our intended 24/7 run to Kodiak. Tom's older daughter Elise came along, too.

Just as we entered Canadian waters I went below to grease the shaft and look the engine room over. I smelled fuel oil and saw plenty of it in the bilge, so I told Tom to shut the engine down. The boat yard people had left some plastic plugs in the block which were leaking. Tom had iron replacement plugs, so we were under way in an hour.

On May 26 we passed through Seymour Narrows, a notoriously dangerous stretch of water off Vancouver Island, considered by many to be the worst hazard to marine navigation on the British Columbia coast. We caught it with the rising tide and went through at fourteen knots instead of the boat's usual eight knots. We had no problems.

On May 27 I had the wheel from one to six that morning when we finally got past Vancouver Island and entered Queen Charlotte Sound. In Hecate Strait, so named because it is shallow with many rocks, and is especially hazardous in storms and violent weather - all leading to shape-shifting - as the Greek Goddess was know for doing. It got very rough and wild during our passage, so Tom turned east and we found a suitable anchorage for the night up Rivers Inlet.

The attractive Hog Rocks lighthouse near the Alaska/Canada border.

While on watch close to shore I kept my mind and eyes open for a glimpse of a white black bear, or Kermode bear, but I did not spot one.

In the meantime, the people at the boat yard had assured us the water tank was full, but we ran dry. Luckily, as I did on deer hunting trips, I had stashed two five gallon jugs below, along with new doors for my house and a used Honda 110 ATC, so we had coffee water.

Canada and the United States were quarreling over some salmon fishing issues, so we could not legally go ashore on Canadian territory. We got by with what we had- otherwise, we would have gone in to fetch fresh water.

We got into Ketchikan late on May 29 and filled the fresh water tank before tying up at one of the several harbors. At the top of the ramp from the dock was a conveniently located bar, so I bought a six pack of Coors and we all went to bed.

In the morning I went to a hardware store for a few items. Tom found a replacement water pump for the one that had burned out due to low water in the tank. He installed the pump and we departed at mid afternoon.

My best memory of Ketchikan is the five large cruise ships, each of which disgorged thousands of tourists into the little town. Rope cordons were set up to channel the visitors toward the curio shops. I was reminded of rodeo bulls being driven by men with electric prods. The locals I talked with were not happy with so many tourists. Property taxes had risen so high, many locals had moved away, Many shops and homes were taken over by Californians, Hindus and - worst of all, Muslims.

We could see the lights of Wrangel and I was reminded that we were just another ship passing in the night. We got a good view of Kate's Needle as we traveled north. Chatham Strait seemed to take half of forever to get through, though the sea conditions were mild.

Throughout Southeast Alaska, steep, heavily forested mountains rise abruptly from the sea, with few beaches. I have never cared for that part of the state.

We put into Elfin Cove, with a population about fifteen people, where we fueled up at $2.65/gallon and added water. It's an interesting, tiny village where the locals dump their garbage on the beach and wait for the tide to take it away.

Heading north as we tried to round Cape Spencer, we hit some extremely rough water which dislodged Tom's big tool chest from its temporary position on the galley bunk. We turned around and found an inside bay to anchor for the night.

June 2 was rough traveling all day. We passed Lituya Bay where the great earthquake of 1964 washed out trees to a maximum elevation of 1,720 feet (524 meters) above sea level at the entrance of Gilbert Inlet.

I listed twenty significant defects on the boat since it was released from the boat yard, but Tom had managed them all - some only temporarily. The auto pilot kept quitting, the running lights were not functioning and the PA system was out. Those and other problems would be dealt with in Kodiak.

We started across the northern Gulf of Alaska directly to Kodiak, but the GPS quit and the sea got big, so we headed for Middleton Island where we jogged on the lee side for about twelve hours in twenty to thirty foot seas. The radio quit, so Dooley used the Satellite Phone and got the forecast, which was for more bad conditions. We were approximately two hundred kilometers from Kodiak.

In the late 1960s Reeve Aleutian Airlines (I always wondered if they were Revolutionary?) was taking DC3 loads of Anchorage hunters to shoot rabbits on Middleton, but I did not manage to make a trip. The island is about 2km by 8km. It is covered by grasses and mosses, with low elevation and rapidly eroding cliffs since the 1958 earthquake which registered 9.2 on the Richter scale. Its Indian name is "Achakoo" meaning 'without harbor'.

The primary land mammal on Middleton Island is the introduced European feral rabbit *Oryctolagus cuniculus* population, which originated from four domestic rabbits (3 females and 1 male) that were purposely liberated on the island in the fall of 1954. Their population had grown to an estimated twenty to thirty thousand within ten years - like illegal alien immigrants.

I enjoy hunting and eating rabbits and hares, but I did not find Middleton Island to be an inviting place. However it would be interesting to go sometime by air to hunt European rabbits for a couple of days.

On June 4 it was nearly calm as we started across the Gulf of Alaska heading directly to Kodiak. It got rough again by seven that evening. When we came across Portlock Banks we had 25 knots of wind off the starboard bow and a big sea, however we stayed the course. We sighted Marmot Island about fifty miles out, and arrived in Kodiak just after midday on June 5.

This was my first time to make the trip, Dooley had done it once in the same boat twenty-six years before.

Stress in small aircraft can be intense, but it's usually over in a few minutes. Stress on a boat can last for much longer. It was good to be home.

With guests coming for three booking periods I needed to depart Kodiak in early August, amidst a great run of King and Silver salmon. Its always difficult for me to walk away from hot fishing.

We fished during every decent bit of weather in July and had plenty for the coming winter as well as fish to share with Kotzebue folks and other friends.

Kate with her shark, Bess with a 123 pound halibut and a cart of trolled silver salmon.

But duty calls, in this case for me to depart Kodiak on August 8, at four o'clock in the afternoon. The passage to Homer was flat calm and enjoyable, allowing me to sleep for most of the journey. We were in Homer by seven the next morning and after a slow off-loading, I was on the road to Anchorage by eight thirty. The 212 miles were done in three hours, which was nearly a record for me in the 1999 Ford pickup, but on this trip the number of motor homes was far fewer than normal.

News told us that the space shuttle Discovery landed safely that morning.

After the usual stops in Anchorage to buy food and booze, drop off frozen fish, and this time quite a lot of smoked salmon, I was back on the road by mid afternoon, which with little traffic, allowed me to arrive in Fairbanks by eight that evening. I found no clusters of tourist motor homes.

As I drove I was thinking of how nice it would be to have Ted back as Assistant Guide. I met him years ago when he was a Lieutenant in the National Guard assigned to Kotzebue. He came by my sod shack one evening carrying a guitar. Teresa and I were holed up in miserable rain and fog, waiting for a chance to go to the lodge. I invited Ted in, gave him a beer and shared our popcorn as he sang to us. He was complimentary about my videos which were on sale locally and showed great interest in hunting. I asked if he would like to assist me with hunters. He appeared to nearly turn inside out! YES! I got him a license. He began helping me and did so for several years. He had retired in 2005 as a Colonel, but I still referred to him as Left-tenant. He was to join us as an Assistant Guide this year and would bring his old friend, Ron Phillips.

Wednesday, after coffee and a Fred Meyer doughnut, I taxied the cub to the hanger, drained the pickling oil and replaced it with Chevron 20/50, cleaned the cowling and engine, checked the oil screen - which was clear - then cleaned and reset the spark plugs. I charged the battery, packed the main and tail wheel bearings and installed the radios.

Wild fire smoke was dense and suffocating and forecast to remain so for the next few days, so I did some minor optional things to the super cub and also to the pickup. I bought a few things at yard sales, visited friends and literally "hung fire" from August 12 to 14.

My Assistant Guide, Ted and his friend Ron, who would serve as a packer, were in Kotzebue staying at my sod shack. By telephone I told them to charter up to the lodge, I would pay for it when I got there. I had a bunch of split sheets of plywood to place on the second story, but I wanted to be there for that job myself.

The day after after the charter departed I learned that my first sheep hunter was also in Kotzebue, staying at a local bed and breakfast. I cannot deny that I was motivated to get over there to take care of the guest and get started with the building project.

On Monday the visibility in Fairbanks was a mile and a half and forecast to improve, so I bought fresh fruits and vegetables and loaded up for the trip west. Incoming commercial jets were reporting the top of the heavy smoke to be 5500 feet. I stopped to talk with the people in the Flight Service Station, some of whom I knew from their time in Kotzebue. I told them I would need a Special Clearance to depart on a VFR flight plan to Kotzebue about noon. They affirmed that should be possible.

When noon came I turned around to line the cub up for takeoff, but the visibility had dropped to less than a hundred yards. I called the tower and told them I would be delayed and would call them back when ready. As I sat there the smoke seemed to thin out enough for me to go, so a few minutes later, I got the clearance and took off.

At two hundred feet altitude I wished I had not done it. I could not see anything but grey "blah" from less than two hundred feet above the ground. There was nothing to do but continue on my westerly heading, but Murphy Dome, twenty miles away, rises to 2,890 feet and in the zero visibility I preferred to keep extra airspeed as I climbed on a heading of 220 degrees until well clear of the Dome.

Bottom line when stressed while flying is - as long as you're flying, everything is fine, if you keep your head. It's when you quit flying - especially if you abruptly quit - that things get dangerous.

Shortly after breaking ground I got a call from the Tower advising me to turn to 260 degrees and report leaving the Aerodrome Traffic Zone - two and a half miles from the international airport. I ignored the first call, then the second, but on the third call the operator sounded irritated, so I keyed my mike and made sounds like one hears from a faulty mike. Immediately I got another, urgent call from the tower. Mixed in between my faulty mike noises I said I was having a problem with my microphone jack and was clear of the zone. I did not turn to 260 degrees for another thirty minutes and heard no more from the Tower.

Expecting to be into far better conditions around 5,500 feet, I remained in heavy smoke with visibility of undeterminable distance until I reached broken conditions at 8,500 feet.

Fires were scattered over many miles, but I enjoyed the bumpy tailwind.

As soon as I could see the ground, I snapped a photo. The many intense fires created hot air updrafts, which made the air turbulent.

This was not the most relaxing or pleasurable trip I had ever made, but once I got some half-way decent visibility it wasn't too bad. I landed in Kotzebue at six o'clock after being in the air a bit over six hours. The Flight Service people told me mine was the only flight from Fairbanks that day, the scheduled airlines had cancelled all flights due to poor visibility in heavy smoke. I figured they were smarter than I was.

After securing the plane I rescued my guest, Gary, from the B&B and we got hamburgers, visited a couple of friends and went to bed at my old sod shack. Luckily the shack had been cleaned up by Ted and Ron.

Dall ram hunting in northwest Alaska was closed to all but local subsistence-qualified hunters in 1994. In 1998 agreements were reached between the National Park Service, the Alaska Department of Fish and

Game and the Alaska Federation of Natives to allow twelve permits for rams to go to non-subsistence hunters. Gary and two other guests of mine had been drawn for a sheep permit in 1998, but before the opening date of August 10 arrived, the Alaska native associations reneged on their agreement and objected. So the season was closed again to all but local subsistence hunters. I began legal action as a Plaintiff in what became known as the Bondurant Suit which sued in federal court to maintain equal hunting rights in Alaska for all people, regardless of race, culture, or zip code. When sport hunting again became possible in my area in 2004, Gary applied but was not drawn for a permit, but in 2005 he lucked out.

By morning dense smoke had arrived in Kotzebue. After some of the obligatory visits the next morning to the National Park Service, Alaska Department of Fish and Game and the FAA flight service station, I got Gary to the lodge about three that afternoon. The smoke cleared about eighty miles north of town. I introduced Gary to Ted and Ron, who had spotted a couple of dandy rams. I did Gary's paperwork and headed back to town with an empty forty pound propane bottle and some crushed cans and non combustible garbage from the previous season.

After a morning of administrative chores - the least desirable of all activities connected with guiding - I loaded my grandson Spencer and a refilled propane bottle, tied some ten foot two-by-fours and "Z" strips for siding abutments on the right wing strut and headed back to the lodge. We took a circuitous route up the Kaluktavik River and found some fine bull moose on that little, remote drainage.

When we landed and went to the lodge we found no one, so I fired up the Honda and trailer to haul our freight. Before we had all the stuff to the lodge I saw Ted, Ron and Gary coming up the runway. They looked like they were carrying a load.

The three men headed up into West Bowl early that morning and before noon connected with a beautiful, twelve year old ram, whose horns I guessed at a bit shy of forty inches. Later they taped 39 & 5/8 inches. This was a nice beginning to the fall season. Gary had bad knees and used two canes, so he and Ted were off the mountain behind Ron who carried the heaviest load. It had been an easy hunt, in spite of the rough, rocky place where the ram was hanging out.

Ted and Gary, justifiably pleased with the first animal of the season.

That fine ram is about as good as they get - anywhere - and far more impressive than most sheep. The boys told me the old ram never saw them as they climbed to within two hundred yards of its bed. One well placed shot, and the prize was won. Gary told me he hunted in the Alaska Range, the Wrangel Mountains and other places, but this was the best quality ram he had taken. And it was home grown in my back yard! The total score was 160 and 5/8.

Thursday, August 18, after enjoying Ron's terragon scrambled eggs, I opened the old cabin and got out the split T-111 plywood. I set Spencer to rolling stain onto the sheets in plus fifty degree weather and bright sunlight.

Ron and Gary went fishing for the afternoon, while Spencer and I worked on the siding.

On Friday weather was clear and visibility unlimited at Trail Creek so I headed to Kotzebue to pick up an incoming guest, but encountered ground fog half way to town. I flew over Kotzebue at fifteen hundred feet looking for a break in the heavy fog, but found none, so I went back to the lodge. That was three hours of flying for nothing. Henceforth I would call for conditions on the satellite phone.

The next day with slightly better flying conditions I got to town around noon. I topped off my wing tanks and filled the 32 gallon belly tank to take extra fuel to the lodge. My guest Scott was relieved to see me. We made it back to Trail Creek where I syphoned off forty gallons of aviation fuel and returned to town.

My Assistant Guide from the previous year, Mike, was ready to go but we could not get out of town until the next morning. I had a message from my best German friend, Ulrich, that the hunter coming with him had trouble with the Bureau fo Tobacco and Firearms on importing his rifle. I told him not to worry as I had a spare.

The flight with Mike was uneventful. We landed with his large back pack on the left wing strut and some eight foot lumber on the right side. We had seen seven single grizzlies, one of which was huge, lying on the Bear Stairs a mile north of the lodge.

Ted, Ron and Scott were after a ram on the south east slope of the valley near the South Overlook. As I was grilling teriyaki marinated caribou on the fire we heard one shot. I sent Spencer with my .44 magnum pistol to help pack in the meat. The three men were back with a big ram at one o'clock in the morning.

August 22: I caped and salted Scott's ram, then rolled a second coat of stain on the siding - much easier to do before we nailed it onto the second story. With Swede saw and hedge trimmers Spencer, Mike and Scott worked at trimming the high willows on the north end of the main runway.

Scott's ram had the most massive body of any sheep I had seen.

We had a lot of things going on. The hunting and building projects were all going well.

From the window, Gary spotted two grey and one black wolf as they walked into Break Ankle Canyon. I took Scott and watched for a couple of hours in hope of a shooting opportunity, but none came.

About mid-afternoon eighty to a hundred caribou passed down Trail Creek. There were no big bulls, so I had Spencer shoot two barren cows. He wanted the meat to give to family and friends.

A thin thread of caribou with one good bull.

Just before dark a band of caribou, including some impressive bulls passed down the west side of the valley. Shortly after their passage the three wolves showed up. The lobos sat on the highest mogul on the west side and began howling and barking. We were blessed with an impressive serenade which began just before dark and continued for almost an hour. It seemed the big black wolf did most of the howling while the the grays barked. I had the impression they were calling the rest of the pack together in response to the presence of caribou.

The next morning the wolves were still visible on the western moguls and they gave an occasional howl, which puzzled me. It was uncharacteristic behavior.

A small string of caribou came down the west side, so I took Gary across the river and we posted in anticipation of a shot at a good bull or, better still for Gary, a wolf. But wolves are smart and seldom cooperative. When we got positioned, the gang of five wolves stood up, stretched, and trotted north, well out of shooting range.

We held our position and in less than an hour Gary spotted a bull he wanted. With a three hundred yard shot, he anchored the animal.

Ted, Ron and Scott had walked south and Scott got a couple running shots at a gray wolf just off the end of the main runway, but no lead connected with the critter. Later I heard a couple shots from down that way as I was packing Gary's caribou meat.

The boys were back at the lodge by nine that evening with the super fine caribou Scott had downed.

The next day Gary needed to get to town. I drained ten gallons of gasoline out of the cub and loaded up with Gary, his gear, a hundred pounds

2005 Another Exceptional Year

Gary's rack to be prepared in the European style.

Scott and his well balanced, high scoring caribou rack, at 399 points.

of prime game meat, two sheep heads, and four capes in the back and one set of caribou antlers tied on the right wing strut. It was windy from the southeast at twenty gusting to twenty-eight miles per hour, and turbulent, but that's nothing out of the ordinary for Northwest Alaska. I got the two sheep heads checked by the Department of Fish and Game, then packaged and placed the meat in my big chest freezer. I took a caribou hind quarter to the local judge and enjoyed a glass of merlot with him and his wife, then Gary and I hit the sack at midnight.

I woke up at two thirty with a sharp pain in my left heel. It felt like a piece of jagged glass was imbedded in my flesh, but there was no sign of trauma. I stopped by the hospital at eight o'clock. The Indian Health Service physician told me I had *Plantar Fasiitis* - oh, dandy! She prescribed a massive dose of Ibuprofen, which seemed to dull the pain, but every time I stepped on my heel I felt severe, sharp pain. I got by pretty well ignoring it, as I have always done with most pain and discomforts.

Ted left a phone message telling me that Scott needed to be on the plane the next day. I understood he would be with us until Aug.29. Well, this would give me an opportunity to get some grandkids up to the lodge for a few days. After getting Gary to the airport I loaded the cub and took one granddaughter, Shontai, up to the lodge. It would be her first time in years to see the lodge. It was a very turbulent flight, but Shontai endured it in fine shape. When we landed Scott had taken another huge caribou with a score of 396,

My foot only gave me pain when I let the heel touch the ground, so as long as I tip-toed around, it wasn't too bad. I felt creepy walking that way. Its a good thing I didn't have a limp wrist, too!

Scott and I got to town at noon. I gave a hind quarter of sheep meat to a Guide and Transporter friend, Brad Saalsaa. Scott checked in for the jet and I bought some groceries. The wind had picked up to thirty and gusting, so I went back to check my tie downs before going to my daughter Sandy's for dinner.

Saturday, August 27 was nice in Kotzebue and Ted called to tell me the weather was good and winds light at the lodge, so I loaded up groceries and two grandkids, Scarlett and Seth, for their first trip to the lodge.

Our flight was uneventful. However the rapid and dramatic changes in the colors of the leaves and tundra were astounding. In just one day the

2005 Another Exceptional Year

Ron and Scott with Scott's two big bulls.

Scarlett, Seth and Shontai wasted no time assembling a teeter-tooter.

entire country was wearing a different set of colorful foliage apparel.

Progress on the second story siding was satisfactory and the boys had seen a large black wolf on the west moguls, but no chance for a shot came. The grandkids were having a wonderful time at the lodge.

Mike had to depart, his time at the lodge was short, but it would satisfy his requirements as he worked toward his own Registered Guide license. We landed in town at 6pm, to find a strange airplane in my tie-downs, so I used a vacant tie- down. Taking another's tie-downs and ropes is very rude, I would look for the person the next day. I was in time to meet my good friend Ulrich and his companion Rudiger from Germany. Tom Minter and his son, Cody, were due in the next day.

So, on August 29, a scheduled charter day, I sent Ulrich, Tom and Cody in the Cessna 206 to the lodge, along with their gear, rifles, and food. My three grandkids came back to town, along with the last of the fresh meat, on the return leg of the charter. Once the kids were delivered and the meat wrapped and put in the freezer, Rudiger and I flew to the lodge. Days like the last two in town are far more tiring to me than any full day hunting sheep or packing moose meat. We saw three grizzlies south of the lodge, including one huge bear. Rudiger had the only grizzly permit.

The radio told us that Hurricane Katrina made landfall in Louisiana, with 125 mph (200 km/h) winds, making it a strong Category 3 storm.

August 30 began with a warm forty degrees and a north wind of fifteen knots. As Ron was making biscuits and gravy, I took Rudiger to sight in my spare .300 Winchester, since he was unable to bring his own. He was a careful, competent marksman, as I have found most Germans to be.

We had just begun to swallow our tasty breakfast when we sighted a band of caribou across the river heading south at a leisurely pace. Ted and Ron took Rudiger and hustled to intercept the ambling animals.

They crossed the main channel, which was running at low level this season, and wound their way through the willows and cottonwoods along the north side of West Bowl Creek. With the north wind in their face they watched the caribou as they continued toward them with the wind on their tails. At about one hundred yards, Rudiger placed a bullet in the neck of

Rudiger with his first Alaskan trophy caribou.

the best bull and it fell onto its nose, stone dead.

Rudiger was overjoyed at the rack carried by this bull. It far surpassed any fallow deer or red deer he had taken in decades of hunting in Germany. "Lovely, lovely," he said over and over again.

The three men were back with meat and trophy in time for another cup of morning coffee.

The previous season, 2004, had seen large groups of caribou, and now this year was developing with better than average numbers. More important, this year the percentage of large, older bulls was much higher. In some years we do not spot a single bull with antlers that score four hundred points, but this year we were seeing racks of that quality every day.

After a light lunch, Ron and Ted took a quick nap. I continued staining the last of the new siding and began painting the window trim. Near the large window in the main room of the cabin was a willow root that interfered with the ladder which I needed to use to paint the window trim. I decided to chop off that root. Spencer brought me the single bit Hudson Bay ax. He noticed the head was loose and began to tap the head on a flat rock. I told him I'd show him the proper way to do that. Rather than tap the ax head, I tapped the end of the hickory handle, but on the first strong tap, the handle sheared. The hardwood pierced the palm and came out the top of my right hand. I was shocked. Spencer looked nauseous. I pulled the wood out and told Spencer to go siphon a cup of gasoline from a barrel. The ax handle showed dried blood, caribou hair and other contaminants. My wound needed to be cleaned and disinfected.

When I withdrew the splintered handle, a flap of flesh loosely covered the site. I got a set of surgical scissors and told Spencer to snip the flap off, but he was reluctant to do it. It was my right hand and I am right handed so I awoke Ron to cut off the flap. I used "q tips" soaked in gasoline to clean the wound, as I had no other cleanser. I bandaged my hand, and assisted Spencer as he chopped out the root and painted the window trim. I took one Zithromax antibiotic capsule that evening.

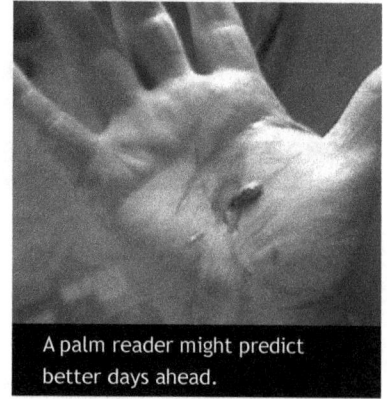
A palm reader might predict better days ahead.

Injuries to the palmar surface are prone to infection, but mine healed quickly and with minimal swelling and discomfort, which, I am sure, was due to the use of gasoline on the dirty wound. I had used gasoline this way on previous occasions.

The new guy, Ron, proved to be pretty all-around handy and a fine cook, too. He made blackened halibut for dinner which especially impressed the Germans.

In the morning my hand was not at all painful, but I changed the bandage and swallowed another Zithromax antibiotic capsule. As the last of the pancakes were put on the table, a band of several dozen caribou were crossing the runway. Ted took Tom and Cody and they shot two good bulls. Tom was enjoying watching his son do most of the shooting.

Normally I keep a small stockpile of fermented libations on hand, but wine does not keep well in the super cold winters at Trail Creek, so the season supply must be brought in with the food in August. We had started with

2005 Another Exceptional Year

Cody with his first Alaskan trophy, off the end of the main runway.

six boxes, each with five liters of wine and suddenly we were on the last box. People having fun do tend to consume more than their usual amount.

Grizzly season opened September first. I took Ulrich and Rudiger north, while the rest of the gang went to the South Overlook. We spotted a dark grizzly feeding on one of the gut piles across the valley from the lodge, but we soon lost sight of it. With several gut piles around, I felt confident that we would find that bear again, as well as several others we'd recently seen. I hoped to find one particular giant bruin I'd been seeing for years.

More than a hundred caribou passed down Trail Creek this day, but none were taken. The boys sighted a wolverine on the east moguls. We dined on barbecued ribs, baked potatoes and salad.

Large, spawning Arctic Char in Dipwater Creek

The berry crop this season was better than average for all species - Blue, Crow, Cran and Soap berries. It was too warm to wear gloves, so most of our group showed large dark splotches on their hands, acquired when they sat down in blueberries to glass for game. There were some suspicious rorschach - like stains on the back sides fo their pants, as well.

September 2 was another beautiful day with temperatures in the high thirties and a light north wind. Ulrich and Rudiger went up stream to make photographs of Char, which are especially beautiful in spawning colors.

Spawning Char, many of over thirty inches in length, and some up to fifteen pounds, visit the upper reaches of Trail Creek every year.

Tom, Cody and Ted went to the top of the eastern moguls to spend a leisurely afternoon glassing for game and soaking up sunshine. Ron and Spencer went to the western moguls in hope of getting some footage for use in the annual promotional video.

I stayed back to work on the siding and trim. I was getting great help from Ron, Ted and Spencer, but I didn't want to abuse them by not doing as much of the scut work as possible, plus my plantar fasciitis still felt like a razor blade on my heel.

Coming home after a sunny day in the field.

2005 Another Exceptional Year

The north wind in late summer and fall usually brings us caribou from the north slope. Caribou are the only prey species I know of that typically walks down wind. I believe this is because they depend on their eyesight more than their noses to keep them from natural predators. It works well for human hunters who are aware of this characteristic of the tundra deer.

With the rest of the hominids from camp all out in pursuit of quadrupeds or fish, I sat on my old sawbuck in brilliant sunshine and enjoyed a quiet cup of coffee. The past several days had been very active - hectic some might say - but productive and satisfying. I had a moment to reflect on it all.

Actually I was living a dream ... a dream I had as a boy to be in the wilderness, acting as a professional hunter. True, there were no lions, hyenas or rhinoceros to deal with. Nor were there hostile Indians or lurking Mau-mau savages to battle physically. I had no string of gun bearers, cooks and camp tenders, beaters and trackers - but my God! I felt lucky, no better than that... I felt generously blessed.

Me, at age 63, with four children, guiding in Alaska for nearly forty years, flying my own airplane, owning eighty acres in a national preserve, having no mortgage or other bills and with a little money in the bank. Yeah, me, the kid who at age 14 was told he had a bad heart and should avoid strenuous physical activity and become a book worm! I could feel the rays of sunlight warming my cheeks. The sun seemed brighter. Yes, I'm a richly blessed, wonderfully privileged person.

Using my home-built extension ladder I brushed stain on the spots that needed it and gave the window trim another coat of oil-based paint. Interestingly enough, the exterior wood seems to deteriorate less in the Arctic with winter temperatures of sixty below zero than wood in dry desert areas, nevertheless the wood needs either stain or paint if it is to last.

As I turned to descend the ladder I saw Tom and Cody coming off the east slope with a springy gait. They were walking on their toes. Tom had something in his back pack. When they strode into the yard Cody gave out a whoop as his Dad opened his pack. Cody had taken a beautiful male wolverine.

As this photo shows, tundra colors in August overwhelm my descriptive ability.

As the father and son sat on a high point glassing up and down the valley looking for caribou, they noticed movement in the willows near a

ALASKA CARIBOU

Cody and his wolverine. The lodge is over his head, half a mile away.

Rudiger, Cody, Ulrich and me with Cody's unique trophy.

small glacial lake below their position. A wolverine was humping around the edge of the water catching voles. It took a couple of full magazines, but the wolverine seemed oblivious to the shooting and eventually one of Cody's lead missiles caught the fierce little predator in the neck. There was minimal damage to the beautiful hide.

Wolverine are the least frequently taken big game animal in Alaska. Most hunters do not even see one.

It was blowing hard in the morning with gusts of over forty miles per hour that made the wind sock stand straight up. Ron was a Boeing 747 pilot for Northwestern Airlines and he needed to get to town that day, but we needed to let the wind diminish a bit before I would fly.

The wind did tire out some by 4pm, so I tied on two sets of caribou antlers, put Cody's wolverine skin and four hind quarters along with Ron and his gear in the cub and headed for town. With a stiff tail wind we landed in an hour and ten minutes.

Sandy and her daughter Jamie met us at the cub. She was upset, as the Federal Aviation Administration had been calling everyone, including Teresa in Kodiak. They reported me three days late on a flight plan, but my notes indicated I was three hours early. FAA was about to scramble a USAF Hercules to begin a search, but one of the old hands at the Kotzebue Flight Service Station mentioned that I had never been late and insisted they check their voice recordings. Sure enough, I was not late. Someone had misread the notes and did not double check. Too many government people are less than dependable!

I got Ron a quick sandwich and put him on the jet, wishing him well and telling him he is welcome to return any time. After supper at Sandy's I gave caribou meat to several people and hit the sack tired.

The north wind was still strong at twenty gusting to thirty when I departed for Trail Creek. I put in an extra ten gallons of gas and the trip took over two hours. I had one wing strut loaded with eight foot 2X4 lumber and a damaged aluminum extension ladder on the other side. A contractor that was leasing a lot from me said I could have the ladder if I got it out of town before his people destroyed it. It would be handy at the lodge. I added twenty gallons of fuel oil to make a decent load.

The wind at Trail Creek was still out of the northeast and gusty, so I used the cross wind strip and was stopped in less than one hundred feet. I unloaded and learned that I had missed another hunt for a great animal.

Ted had taken Rudiger less than a mile from the lodge to shoot a heavily palmated caribou - one of the most attractive I had ever seen.

Also during my absence, Spencer had taken Cody across the river and connected with a dandy big bull.

The hunting was producing some extraordinarily fine trophies, but I

Rudiger and his long tined, well palmated bull. It placed #2 in the state.

This fine bull would win the #3 Caribou award for 2005 for Cody. Our guests took all three top caribou awards this year.

Cody's two big bulls and Rudiger with his first one.

was spending more time in logistics than I preferred. Nevertheless, things were coming together nicely and I was pleased.

For supper I fried caribou back strap, boiled potatoes and Spencer made a green salad. Everyone missed Ron's cooking.

I had not seen a snowshoe hare hereabouts since 1980, but Ted said he saw a hare. I asked where and he reported the hare was near the out house.

"Oh yeah, a pubic hair, no doubt," was my reply.

But Ted was adamant. He had seen a snowshoe hare. The next day I saw one, as well. This is wonderful to have the bunnies back. We deferred shooting any until the next season. I prefer deep fried hare or rabbit to chicken.

Just before dark we watched a Snowy owl cruise the swamp east of the lodge. The large bird made two landings which I assume indicated he nailed a vole or lemming, but in the dim light we could not be certain of that. Short Eared Owls are commonly seen from the windows, but Snowy Owls are rarely seen here in September.

Beginning around ten o'clock that evening we were entertained by an extraordinary display of northern lights. The Aurora was bright, colorful and active on both sides of the valley. I went to bed after watching half an hour, but my guests remained enthralled for two hours or more.

With the lights and presence of abundant caribou, I expected the wolves to tune up, but they were silent. Most likely they were out of howl range.

September 6 began with a light north wind and clear conditions. I took Tom and Cody to the South Overlook. We saw scattered bands of caribou all day. A blond grizzly sow with a nearly white cub munched their way through several blueberry patches along the western foothills. We made a long day of the trip, returning after eight thirty. Spencer had applied another coat of paint to the window trim and he'd put the turkey in the oven at noon. The bird was delicious with mashed potatoes and gravy.

There were many lemmings this year, which kept the owls and weasels in active pursuit. One of the fellows caught one of the diminutive rodents. It was very quiet and non-agressive. Ulrich told him the little critter would die of stress if kept too long, so it was released.

Ted had a head cold, so I gave him some Vitamin C and told him to take it easy. He was using the small cabin, so was less apt to contaminate the rest of us. Viruses spread quickly in lodge situations like this.

A medium sized dark grizzly was hanging around a kill site across the river from the lodge. Rudiger was scheduled to depart soon and he wanted to take the bear.

The kill site was in open tundra with very large hummocks which rose up two to four feet from their bases. After topping out on the cutback which outlined the course of the river, we crawled on hands and knees to one of the hummocks which was about one hundred and fifty yards from the bear. The bear would disappear from view for a few minutes, then show up again, sniffing the wind and looking about before getting back down to business with the caribou remains. It's actions suggested it was a sub-dominant bear. We set up on a large hummock which overlooked a shallow swale which had shallow standing water between the hummocks. I saw no need for us to get wet by crawling any further. I got Rudiger comfortable in a prone rest on the hummock, then I let out a wolf howl.

The bear immediately rose and stood on top of a large hummock, again sniffing and looking right and left. It looked angry. Its left side offered a nearly perfectly angled shot and Rudiger placed a bullet just behind the shoulder. The bear turned and tried to bite the shot - the usual reaction. I told Rudiger to put another one in him, but he was slow to respond and the bear turned and ran to the west. Rudiger fired three more times, hitting the bear twice before it dropped out of sight behind some small willows.

My German guest was excited about this animal. When we came to the carcass we walked around to approach it from uphill. I noted that the eyes were open in a fixed stare. The bear was dead.

Just across the river from the lodge. Those in the lodge watched the stalk.

This twelve year old sow had a serious wound at the base of her nose.

I have seen similar wounds on bears killed by other bruins. Most of this type of injury are found in younger bears killed by older boars to eat. I assume it is the final, killing bite. But I had never seen damage like this in a living healthy bear. I assumed this had taken place in a mating struggle the previous May or June, however when I saw the cleaned and bleached skull, the bone repair indicated it was a much older wound - the sow had lived with this injury for a least two or three years. This bear was healthy and carried plenty of fat.

Once again I observed Rudiger revert from his normally reserved self to a younger person, full of awe and ecstasy at talking this fine trophy. I've seen this temporary metamorphosis many times in hunting guests and I am sure that those who do not undergo at least some change of this nature have lost something precious. Those who do not hunt may never experience it.

The day remained lovely with a gentle northerly breeze and temperature rising to a high of plus thirty-six degrees. I carefully skinned the beast to avoid spending extra time fleshing it at the lodge. Rudiger gave me good help by pulling the skin as I cut it free from the underlying fat. Ulrich came over to visit and assist as well.

Back at the lodge Ted was feeling better and helped me remove the feet from the bear hide, then he cleaned up the skull.

Spencer had taken Tom and Cody out but saw only a few small caribou all day.

I cobbled together a turkey stew, then after listening to the weather broadcast which I picked up at the airplane on the Non Directional Beacon, I decided to take Rudiger to town the next day, as a big storm was headed our way.

Morning fog reduced visibility to an eighth of a mile. We sat as conditions gradually improved. I called the flight service station in Kotzebue at noon and decided to take Rudiger to town. I had to fly a bit off direct course to avoid patches of low visibility, but after getting a Special Clearance to enter the zone, we landed before six that evening.

The hams of this bear were fine eating - tender and tasting like beef.

The big storm came earlier than predicted. It was the end of a typhoon from southeast Asia, which is not unusual to see in northwest Alaska in the fall.

Weather was down in the morning, but I got a "Special" and headed up for Ulrich - of course with a bunch of lumber and cans of stove oil to make a full load. Again it was a touchy/feely flight with strong wind and turbulence, but I landed on the cross wind strip and was stopped after only a few revolutions of the wheels. Ulrich was ready, so I loaded up with caribou and bear meat and we were off, this time with a strong tail wind all the way to town.

Ulrich and Rudiger departed on the first jet flight the next morning. It always sad to see my special friend, Ulrich, depart. We have hunted together a dozen times in Alaska and several times in West Germany, then in the reunified Germany.

I loaded the Cessna 206 charter with a used Honda 110 ATC to be used for spare parts on my two 1979 machines. Those wonderful machines were becoming scarce. The pilot picked up Tom, Cody and the rest of the meat and headed for town.

After seeing the two Florida guests off, I spent a stormy night in Kotzebue, then was able to get a clearance to go back to the lodge the next day. It was another windy, turbulent trip, but as is so often the case, the wind at ground level was much less than that at higher elevations.

Spencer and I would have a week or so to peck around at little projects at the lodge and perhaps do some hunting for ourselves. The weather remained undecided as is common in spring and fall - times of the equinox. Some days we had dense fog until past midday. We got a lot of rain, but caribou were still dribbling through and we made a nice stalk on a good bull for Spencer.

On the thirteenth we were beset again with heavy fog and drizzle. As I was frying bacon at mid-morning Spencer glassed a huge bear coming our way from Three Mile Ridge. This great beast was walking in a manner I had never before seen a bear travel. It seems to be stomping its feet. Every few yards it would stop and swipe out a chunk of tundra. It looked extremely angry, as if having a tantrum. This was the giant we had seen for years, but had never got a chance to shoot.

As Spencer had not taken a bear yet, I asked him if he would like to get this one.

"Yeah, Grandpa. Both of us, uh?"

So I stopped with breakfast, we booted up and made for the far end of the runway. The massive bear had been lost from our view since he entered the riparian growth

Spencer and another nice caribou.

near the river. I was hoping to see him emerge from the willows and come toward the large open area that contained the runway. The drizzle matured into a heavy rain. With wet lenses we returned to continue our vigilance from the lodge.

I had seen such a bear on several occasions over the last four years and occasionally came upon some huge paw prints, but we never were able to put a guest in a shooting situation with that giant bear. It may die of old age.

Rain continued and the creeks were rising. We worked at sawing shed moose antlers for gun racks and hooks and other trivial projects. We read and napped. In breaks between heavy rain we watched snowshoe hares and a weasel thrust and parry in the yard. Eventually the weasel caught an immature hare, killed it and drug it toward its lair under the small building.

The rain continued which produced the highest water levels I had seen in September. It was impossible to cross the main river and some of the side streams were becoming treacherous as well.

I had planned to roll the last of the Behr woodstain on an additional coat on the new siding, but the rain prevented that, so I would have to take the stain back to town to keep it from freezing. The last coat would go on next season.

Spencer had graduated from high school this year. In a big deer contest I had won a new Winchester Model 70 chambered in .280 caliber. I asked Spencer if he would like to have that or a new Model 70 in .300 Winchester Magnum. He chose the .280, so it was his as soon as I could get it to him.

On September 17, with decent flying conditions reported in Kotzebue, we closed up the lodge and out buildings and called an end to the season. It had been a dandy season. We had great weather for most of the time our guests were in camp. I had Ted, Ron and Spencer to help with the siding and guiding, which was especially important for the few days my plantar fasciitis was so troublesome. I had given three grand children a few days at the lodge and the quality of trophies taken was excellent. We harvested sixteen big game animals at Trail Creek this year, one Grizzly, two Dall rams and thirteen Caribou.

September 23. A fierce wind of up to 50 miles per hour was blowing in Kotzebue, so I did paperwork for the Alaska Department of Fish and Game and interviewed potential renters for the sod shack, finally picking one.

2005 Another Exceptional Year

Monday, September 26 finally produced conditions good enough for me to attempt a VFR flight to Fairbanks. I got out of Kotzebue before noon and landed in at Chena Marina at 5:45pm. It was an uneventful flight.

After winterizing the cub with secure tie downs, pickling oil, an engine cover and covers over the main wheels, the next day I was headed for Anchorage about 3pm. Doing 70 to 90mph I was there by 8pm. There was little traffic, but the threat of a love smitten moose on the road is real in September, especially when driving in the dark. I saw no moose this trip.

The National Rifle Association had a meeting in Anchorage that week and the next day my friend Wayne Anthony Ross (WAR), one of the Board of Directors, invited me to join the tour to Whittier and College Fjord, so I went along and had a good time.

After the trip on the *M/V TUSTUMENA* I arrived home on September 30, but hunting wasn't done for the year. Tom Dooley and I had several guests to Transport to the south end of Kodiak to hunt deer.

On November 8 we headed south on the *F/V REBEL* toward Kaguyak Bay. The wind was nasty at thirty-five to fifty miles per hour and though it was mainly offshore, the surf was too high to put anyone on the beach, so we motored on to Russian Harbor, where we stayed at anchor for two days due to the stiff wind. About a foot of snow had accumulated, with some drifts of over three feet.

Our guests for this trip were four veterinarians, including one young fellow I had known for about twenty years. I picked their brains regarding cryptorchidism and sterility in females. I shot a couple of does, primarily to receive instruction on female internal anatomy. The ovaries are found bilaterally near the entrance to the fallopian tubes and are very small. If the animal has ovulated, the ovary will show a scar, indicating the doe is fertile. The does I harvested were apparently fertile.

These vets were all long-time deer hunters and they began taking some very impressive trophies. All of the bucks taken were bilateral cryptorchids - sterile animals. I was collecting femoral blood from which I separated - then froze the serum, the undescended testis, gubernacula, a piece of meat, a sample of fat, some hair with follicles attached, an anterior tooth, and various other samples for the study I was conducting with Colorado State University. I needed some normal, fertile bucks to provide control samples.

On Sunday, November 13, I dropped the hunters off on the beach, then began my own hunt. I spotted a bunch of about sixty deer with what appeared to be a large, normal three X three at the back. I wanted that buck. When the buck paused on a ridge with open ground on both sides, I took a shot and dropped the deer. When I got to the spot, I found only hair and a speck of blood. My bullet had creased the top of the spine which knocked the buck down, but he got up and ran. I saw the animal running below me along a small stream, so I lead it a bit and dropped him.

As I was in pursuit of the deer I crossed large fresh bear tracks which were going upwind from my route. The close presence of a bear had me a bit twitchy, as I had to take samples, cut and load the meat of the deer before going back to the beach. Bears can home in on a single shot. I had fired twice. The deer was lying close to some alders at the base of a small hill. I gathered my samples as quickly as I could and was tying the last quarter of the meat on my pack frame when I looked up and stared in the face of a huge bear! This massive beast was fifteen yards and slightly uphill from me. I believe the bear was a surprised as I was.

Uncontrollably I shouted, "GOD," then "No, No, No" as the bear slowly walked toward me. I was stuck on NO, NO, as I jacked another round into the chamber of my rifle.

If the bear had rushed me I would likely have been unable to get a shot off, but the animal came very slowly and did not make eye contact with me. I resolved to shoot it in the head if it speeded up or looked me in the eye.

With me still shouting NO, NO, NO the bear walked to the gut pile at my feet - so close I could have touched it from where I stood - it paused, then turned and slowly walked away.

When the bear got on the other side of the nearby alders it began to pop its jaws - making a sound like two bricks being slammed together. I quickly put my pack on, grabbed my bag of samples and the head, then backed away. But I fell backward and realized my rifle was chambered and not on safe. What a way to shoot my own foot off! I rose and backed away as the bear came in and began sniffing and eating what I had left of the deer. When I was a hundred yards distant I sat down and realized I had dropped my reading glasses at the kill site. I was content for the bear to have them.

Thirteen had always been a lucky number for me and today, November 13, was another confirmation of that.

We completed our last Transported deer hunt on December 3 and the rest of the year was spent on routine family activities.

Chapter Twelve

A Hoax and Reversal of Fortune

A few years back we entertained a delightful group of four Belgian big game hunters. Two of the men were brothers and the other two were married to sisters of the first two, making them brothers-in-law. These doubly cross-matched relatives enjoyed joking with, and disparaging each other, always in good taste. They had decades of experience in that sort of scamming, so the job had grown tougher over the years. These guys were calloused and experienced. For one of their own to put one over on these guys would be difficult - to say the least.

Early the first evening they each made a significant contribution to the "best animal" pot. The most impressive animal of any species taken by a group member would win the several hundred dollar pot.

As the fifteen-day booking progressed, one of the brothers-in-law, John, seemed to be consistently coming up short on trophy quality. His grizzly was a bit smaller than those of the others. He did not take a dall ram. The Arctic Char and Grayling he landed were somewhat smaller than the fish of his peers. He had not yet collected a wolf. Even the Willow Ptarmigan he shot were not so fine as those of his companions - or so the others claimed. The others were diligent in pointing out the differences between his trophies, the "minnows" he landed and the birds he dropped and those of his companions. According to comments by the others, John typically got the small stuff. Woe be unto poor John.

John bore his position with dignified resignation. It was clearly turning out to be "his turn in the barrel." He went about his time seemingly assured that his day would eventually come.

There was an especially abundant crop of "Alaska cotton" (*Eriophorum*) that year, which I mentioned to John. He was a milliner and knew his cotton.

Rubbing it between his fingers, he told me it would make the finest cloth imaginable if it could be economically collected in large enough amounts. He gathered up a large handful and rolled it between his palms to produce a string, or thread of the material. Yes, he said it was a pity that this wonderful plant was not modified to become commercially valuable. I was fascinated by John's comments and the fine quality of our wild cotton, but one of his brothers-in-law heard John's comments and suggested that John give up hunting wild game and go into pursuing and breeding wild weeds.

John and I were away from the lodge for four days as we pursued, and he eventually took, a capital moose. Just prior to the group's departure from Europe, the world learned that on August 18, 1991, Soviet President Mikhail Gorbachev had been placed under house arrest. Things looked dicey in Mother Russia. Huge political change was looming in the USSR. It appeared to be a military coup and many pundits speculated about the likelihood of aggressive military action by the Soviets.

During the period John and I were away, smoke from forest and tundra fires in Siberia had been borne by westerly winds to cover most of northern Alaska. It was a unusual weather situation.

As John and I were flying back to the lodge from Kotzebue he suggested we tell the others that the smoke was due to fires in the Soviet Union. That part was already known to all, but he planned to add that two days ago, the Russians had attacked San Francisco and immediately thereafter the United States had retaliated with massive bombing runs on several Russian cities. No nuclear weapons had so far been deployed. The smoke had noticeably increased during our absence, so this helped make his story believable. And once again it appeared that the world was about to be consumed in a massive war.

Broadcast radio reception at the lodge had been especially poor and when it was marginally audible, it was weak and nearly impossible to understand due to static. No one bothered to try to decipher the garbled transmissions. John's intended victims would likely have no knowledge of the real reason the smoke had become thicker. Based as it was on a partial truth, combined with anxiety over the Soviet regime change, his ruse just might work! He reminded me to keep a straight face and not spill the beans regarding the actual situation. I looked forward to this quiet, long-suffering man's bid for revenge.

This was before the days of digital cameras, so John could only describe his fine, sixty-seven inch moose, which he did immediately after we landed, His story was met by doubt and derision. John remained stone-faced as his companions carried on with their familial abuse, which now included casting aspersions regarding his measurement of the moose antlers.

When one of the others asked about the increased smoke, John feigned surprise at the question, saying that surely everyone knew of the Soviet attack on San Francisco, followed immediately by the United States Air Force strikes on Petersburg, Moscow, Petropavlovsk and other major Russian cities. The cold war gone hot was by now old news to most residents of the world, John assured them. He played the group masterfully.

My own employees, Ted and Boris, were taken in by the story. Boris said he counted San Francisco as no great loss as it was heavily populated by homo sexual life forms. The Belgian brothers chuckled at his comment.

All four of these guests had international business interests and we began to hear of potential negative financial consequences they would likely suffer due to a war of world-wide dimension. The three "victims" drew lots to determine which would ride to town with me the next morning on a special flight to check in on their businesses and reassure relatives and friends of their safety.

John offered few comments during this noisy, frenetic discussion. He wanted them to swallow the bait deeply, before he set the hook. He remained serenely silent and contemplative with a sympathetic demeanor, but after a bit, he did suggest that he be the one to go to town. At this, the others all pounced on poor John, admonishing him for not making the appropriate phone calls before returning to the lodge.

John assured everyone that their fears were alarmist and thoroughly unwarranted, only to be curtly contradicted by all three of his companions. They were firmly hooked!

They decided to draw lots to determine which man was to go to town. I suggested that Frederich be the one, as he had not yet been given an opportunity to hunt for a moose.

My suggestion made sense, so Frederich went downstairs to get his travel items ready for an early morning departure.

These fellows normally played cards after dinner, and usually with some pretty high stakes. I noticed that John was winning more than half of the pots, including all the really big ones. And we're talking more than just pocket change. The other men's consternation was evident and probably had a negative effect on their concentration, and therefore, their ability to play cards. John made sure they all observed his immense pleasure in taking their money.

Outside, Ted wondered if the group would decide to stay for their entire booking period. I told him I surely hoped they would and I would bet some money that they would stay the full fifteen days. Ted did not take the wager.

Ted, Boris and I normally headed to bed before our guests. As I made my final trip outside to empty my bladder, John joined me and asked that I say nothing about his hoax until Frederich was in town and ready to place a call to his office. I should let the ruse linger as long as possible. John assured me that he would break the news to the others well after Frederich and I had departed. He wanted to savor his delightful deceit as long as possible. I figured he had earned that.

Upon our arrival in Kotzebue I refilled the fuel tanks on the cub, which made Frederich a bit antsy. He wanted to get to a telephone as soon as possible. I reminded him that Kotzebue time was a full ten hours earlier than Belgium time. He said it didn't matter if he disturbed someone's slumber. We drove to town in my old pickup and he switched on the radio. He said he wondered why the broadcast was not full of war news.

Keeping my guest on the hook any longer would have been difficult and perhaps, even cruel. I didn't know him that well and he was a guest, after all. I told him how John had proposed the swindle and admitted my complicity. It took about three minutes to lay it all out for him.

Frederich's face went blank. He just stared at me, then asked me to repeat what I had just told him. After a few seconds of digesting what he had swallowed the day before, Frederich slapped me hard on the back and began to roar in laughter at his own gullibility. He said he was proud of John's action, which he said was certainly justified and masterfully executed.

Ted told me of the reactions of the others when John fessed up. They showed a strange combination of disbelief, followed by profound relief. Then, John became the hero of the moment, heartily congratulated by all.

This, John told me later, was his finest coup of several he had engineered over the past forty years on family hunting trips.

Frederich and I were blessed with near perfect conditions and he had a fine moose on the ground before noon the next day. His great moose was very good, but a bit less impressive than the one John collected. I flew him, the moose backstraps and tenderloins, the head, and our camp back to town. I got Fredereich and the load to my little cabin, then had time to go back for the last of the meat.

Before dark that same day Frederich and I were enjoying fresh moose tenderloin wrapped with bacon, along with baked potatoes and wine. The main topic was John's skillfully executed hoo-raw, rather than the wonderful trophy Frederich had taken.

The next morning we flew back to the lodge and arrived just as Ted and Boris were about to set off with our guests for the day's hunt. I suggested that John and I go north in the aircraft to look for animals, since I could not guide the day I had flown.

Caribou had not been coming through Trail Creek in great numbers that fall, so I took John to the North Slope to find some. We encountered several hundred animals, including some well antlered bulls just over the pass from Trail Creek to the North Slope, so we returned to the lodge. I expected that large bunch to be near the lodge by morning.

The next morning after seeing no caribou from the lodge windows I walked up the creek with John. I expected the big bunch of caribou we had seen the previous afternoon would have entered the Trail Creek drainage, but I could not spot any.

As we enjoyed our sack lunch near the head of Trail Creek, I detected a movement in the brush across the creek. After several minutes of staring through my binoculars, I realized I was looking at the top points of a large caribou rack. The animal was lying in some low willows just off the main stream. The wind was nearly calm. After crossing the main creek channel, we made an easy stalk and watched until I saw the lower parts of the rack. Its bez and double shovels were as impressive as the upper tines.

We needed only to move a little to give John a clear shot at one of the finest caribou I had ever seen, in my more than thirty years of guiding. The big bull was asleep less than forty yards from our shooting position and upon being struck just behind the head, it merely laid its head over and was dead. It was the only caribou we saw that day!

John's luck was phenomenal! That tundra bull had heavy palmation in the upper beams, the bez, the double shovels, and its symmetry were nearly perfect! Its body was at least thirty percent larger than the average bull. This was a rare monster among Barren Ground Caribou. Any hunter would like to collect a trophy of that quality, but few get the opportunity.

John admiring his magnificent caribou.

None of the group disparaged John's caribou, in fact all seemed awestruck. Some suggested this animal would win the "best animal" pot for John.

Taking such a superb specimen like this early in a booking can be a problem if others in the group expect to collect a comparable beast. I've seen it happen, especially with inexperienced hunters, that they have an opportunity to take a good representative, but turn it down, expecting a genetic giant similar to one taken early in the booking, only to come to the end of their hunt with a much lesser specimen, or no trophy at all. Luckily this wasn't early in the booking and these were all experienced, realistic hunters and were content with respectable, if lesser animals.

The fifteen days had been pleasantly productive for the four Belgians. They had each taken a grizzly, three had bagged a huge moose, two added a Dall ram to their collection, three took one caribou each and one fellow got a wolf. They all thanked me and said it was the best, and most exciting hunt of their life.

And John won the significant monetary treasure for the most impressive trophy animal of the trip.

Chapter Thirteen
A Second Try for Caribou and Grizzly with Jake

I had known Jason Moe for his entire life. In fact, I knew his Dad when Jason's existence was in the form of potatoes and carrots …. maybe garlic, but still in the garden. So we go waaay back.

In 1982 I decided to put another addition on my home/office building in Kotzebue. This was to be a second story addition over the existing main part of the home living quarters. To minimize disruption of home activities we would build a pony wall and support an expanded width of the house with outside buttresses. The project was more demanding than my usual simple plans, so I hired a framing crew from Seattle to come up for a three day weekend to get the job framed in and enclosed. Jason's Dad, Bruce came along with the crew and brought his youngest son.

I could not allow a nice kid like Jason to come so far without at least a fishing trip. So one evening we took the float plane and found some lunker-sized Northern Pike.

Jason was with us next in Y2K when Greg Fischer got severely mauled by a large Grizzly. Jason and the rest of our guests took turns assisting me as we carried and drug Greg from the site of his near fatal mauling to the lodge which was four and a quarter miles away by GPS. The actual distance we covered with Greg was probably closer to six or

Jason, age 8, on the right and a friend in 1982 with some Northern Pike in Kotzebue, Alaska.

eight miles. The route includes some steep side hills and some of the most difficult tussocks and swampy areas in the valley. As Jason was the tallest man in the group, on sidehills he got the downhill side to level out the load.

But with the mauling, along with heavy rains and flooding, Jason did not harvest a caribou or a grizzly.

Fifteen years would pass before Jason got back up to the Arctic to resume his pursuit of big game trophies.

In those many years I had not remembered just how large a fellow Jason had matured to be. I recall this young sprout at age eight, now he was forty-one. As we waited for his luggage I reminded him of how I used to bounce him on my knees as we played rodeo in his Dad's living room. Jason offered to bounce me on his knees - right there. I respectfully declined his offer.

Jason was our first guest hunter of the season and he would initially be the only hunter in camp. This was the first year to not have my own aircraft and Cessna 206 charters had increased to over fourteen hundred dollars each. I figured we could get up in one trip with Ron, Jason and me and enough supplies to last for twelve days. I took more boxes of supplies to the plane that I figured the pilot would carry. It's better to have too much than to waste a freight opportunity. We had to leave three apple boxes full of food in the hanger.

We were seeing large herds of caribou for the last twenty miles of the trip. The groups numbered from dozens to hundreds. Jason was excited. So were Ron and I!

The pilot was in a hurry, as usual, so we rapidly unloaded the plane and he took off. Arriving at the lodge with the first hand load of groceries, I parted the curtains and put the spotting scope on an outstanding bull about a thousand yards down the valley. I showed the animal to Jason and told him I expected that bull, if taken, would place in the top three of the annual competition, but we could not shoot him the same day airborne and he likely would be miles away by the next morning. This bull was easily identifiable as it had only five top points (most capital bulls have seven or more top points), but the first one on each antler was exceptional long. The rack was well balanced and esthetic all around.

Only after all the food and freight had been packed to the lodge did I go about sorting out what food went where, etc. I thought I had distributed the critical items evenly among the boxes, but we found out to our chagrin that all the mayonnaise had been left in Kotzebue! Well, I suppose the old timers either did without or they whipped caribou tallow up for a spread. Maybe we could find out. We did without the mayo.

Ron stewed up a fine pot of chicken and home-made dumplings and we three swallowed an entire pecan pie for dessert. My whiskey supply must have been sitting next to the mayonnaise, but Ron and Jason had bottles and as the host, I could not allow them to drink alone.

Jason was right at the spotting scope looking out the window as soon as he woke up. We had a delightful breakfast of bacon, eggs and toast, entertained by the faint, undisturbed ramblings of hundreds of caribou on both sides of the valley.

Jason's grizzly tag could not be used until September 1 or later, but we scrutinized the terrine looking for bruins, as we evaluated the many mature bull caribou.

We were enjoying these moments of splendor in the pristine wilderness. After about an hour of enjoying coffee and conversation, we decided we might walk up into the East Bowl Moguls and glass the valley from that elevated vantage point. As I made a final scan of the moguls, the big bull that held our attention the evening before loomed into view. With the wonderful antler conformation I was sure it was the same animal and today it was within a few hundred yards of where we saw it last.

There were so many caribou on the hillside, we would have to be cautious as well as lucky to not spook the entire local band of caribou and with that loose the opportunity to harvest that dandy trophy.

We left the lodge with pack boards, rifles, and minimal other items. The swamp to the east of the lodge was crossed quickly and we used the broken terrane to conceal ourselves as best we could. Slow travel and caution were the order of the day. Once we inadvertently startled a cow and calf. The cow jumped, trotted a few yards, looked back at us and went back to munching on lichens as the calf nuzzled and attempted to nurse. With so many caribou in the valley, most of the animals were complacent, but if they smelled us or if any panicked and charged off in a rush, the whole valley might erupt in headlong flight. This was on my mind. I have seen it happen that way.

The target bull had moved off the hillside and was slowly grazing at the edge of the broad alluvial fan. We were stuck at three hundred and thirty yards, as per Ron's rangefinder. If we tried to move closer the chances are we would bugger the peaceful animals. I prefer shots to be much closer than that, but Jason was confident and he sighted in satisfactorily the evening before.

When the bull offered a broadside view, Jason cut loose with a 180 grain Nosler from his .300 Winchester Magnum. Nothing happened. Jason cursed. A few of the caribou closer to us lifted their heads, looked around and went back to feeding. The target bull walked behind some low willows, unconcerned. He was now slightly more than three hundred and fifty yards from our position. The tundra was composed of grassy tussocks and moss, offering no hint of where the missed shot might have landed.

Jason whispered that he didn't know how he could have missed, but that he was going to do it this time. I told him to trust his rifle.

At the sound of his second shot the big bull dropped to the tundra so hard, it looked like he bounced. A short burst of kicks from his hind legs indicated a spine shot. He was anchored.

We sat, taking our time to watch the dynamics below us. It was not mid-morning yet. There was no need for haste.

This bull was in prime fat condition. His steaks would be mouth-watering.

We caped the bull and laid the quarters, back straps and other pieces out to drain on willow branches. We would have only a five or ten minute pack to the edge of the cut bank which was within my patented acreage. The rest of the meat haul to the lodge would be done in the trailer of the three wheeler.

Not only was this kill site handy in that it required only a short pack of the meat and cape, it was visible from the windows of the lodge. We still had a grizzly and hopefully some wolves to harvest, this gut pile might draw a target for Jason.

So this was a wonderful day with a great result and minimal physical exertion. I never disparage the easy ones!

Two years before Ron and I arrived to find the lodge had been broken into and badly torn up by a large grizzly. This was the first such calamity

A Second Try for Caribou and Grizzly with Jake

Jason is pleased this bright day with his dandy bull which won 3rd Place in the annual Big Three Competition.

The lodge can be seen over the left antler.

to befall the two story main lodge. In 1975, a small female Toklat grizzly tore off a piece of siding and tried to enter the small twelve by twelve foot cabin that my wife and I were sleeping in. I shot that bear as it entered the cabin. Repair of the damage was quick and easy. Not so in 2014. Ron and I spent more than three long weeks restoring the two-story lodge and we had the assistance of my son Martin and grandsons Spencer and Stuart for a week on that project.

After claiming ownership by right of conquest sometime in July, on September first, the perpetrator came back to visit his new "den" and one of our guest hunters shot him a couple of feet from the door.

In all, my family and guests have killed more than a dozen grizzlies, by shooting from the windows of the two-story lodge. Though not built for that purpose, the second floor has turned out to be a fine shooting stand for grizzlies.

Ron and Jason were off to the South Overlook the next day, while I did maintenance chores. They spotted a huge grizzly feeding along the main stream, digging out massu roots or eskimo potatoes. The pair spent most of the day maneuvering in the willows and dwarf birch, attempting to get a clear shot at the massive bruin, but their best efforts were to no avail.

Upon arriving at the lodge, Jason removed his boots and showed blisters the size of silver dollars on each heel. He did not complain, but we were all reminded of how important it is to have Moleskin adhesives handy for such occasions.

The next day seemed a good one to remain in or near the lodge. I know very well how painful heel blisters can be. Unfortunately they normally torture a person for well over a week before healing. We needed to give Jason's wounds a chance to firm up a little.

As we were overhauling the lodge after the serious bear damage in 2014, I noticed the wooden frames of the double windows in the kitchen area were showing signs of wood rot. They would need replacement. Luckily, thirty-four years before, I had ordered a second set of windows and they were in storage under a bunk in the small cabin. This seemed an ideal time to replace the big double windows.

So Jason pitched right in and in a couple of hours we had the old set of windows out and the new ones set in place. By opening the window fully, the interior brace could be unhooked and the window brought horizontal, allowing unobstructed shooting with camera or firearm. I carefully lubricated the squeaky cranks of the new set.

So another fine day came to a close. Only the presence of mayonnaise and my whiskey jug could have made it better. We had not yet run out of the fermented juices brought by Jason and Ron, but that prospect was looming.

The next morning as I lit the fire under the coffee pot, Jason joined me. He whispered that a large bear was standing just outside the door. I got to the window and whispered for Jason to go downstairs, get his rifle and load it, as quietly as possible.

Everyone keeps the rifles with magazines full and nothing in the chamber, hanging from pegs in the lower main room.

In bare, blistered feet, Jason eased down the stairs, chambered a round and came back. By then, the bear had walked down the trail to the runway before turning back toward the sauna building. Soon it was standing next to the nearest corner of the sauna, rubbing against the building. This bruin was no stranger to the buildings - it seemed right at home. I eased the new window open, dreading a squeak, but the lubrication was effective and no sound issued from my slow cranking.

Jason stood next to me and lined up on the bear. I'm not sure I even noticed the roar of his big rifle, but the bear felt it! The grizzly jumped straight up and ran into the willows to its right.

Ron was out the door of his bedroom. He no doubt knew, but by reflex he asked "What happened?"

I deferred to Jason to fill Ron in on the quick events of the recent moments.

We all had a cup of fresh perked coffee before walking out in our slippers to check on the bear. It was lying stone still just out of sight in the dense willows between the path to the sauna building and the trail to the airport. It showed no movement.

It looked like this was already another good day after several in a row!

Ron and I made the main cuts, down the belly and each leg before going upstairs for breakfast. Those cuts are easier to keep straight before rigor mortis sets in.

Jason's eyes are glowing almost as much as are those of his grizzly.

We took our time to skin this critter close to avoid as much fleshing later as possible. We had the hide salted and rolled before lunch time.

What a shame the nonresident limit for caribou is reduced to only one as we saw many more worthy bulls.

I hung the bear hams next to the caribou meat and removed the gall bladder to give to some worthy person (its illegal to sell bear galls in Alaska) before dragging the carcass to a clear spot off the end of the runway. We might see a wolf come to it, but I have seen wolves ignore bear carcasses and guts more often than not. It is common to see other bears feast on their own kind, but some show no interest in such acts of cannibalism.

Jason's heels looked bloody and raw - just awful - but I know he would have walked on for days and miles if he had not already taken his trophies.

With only a wolf or wolverine now available for Jason to collect, Ron and I puttered around with minor lodge and yard projects, while Jason kept at the windows using binoculars and spotting scope as he visually scanned the valley.

Snowshoe hares were not plentiful this year and we had seen very few ptarmigan, or we would have been out in pursuit of the small game.

Jason's unique mount with glaring eyes.

With Jason's heels scabbing over, it was providential that he spend some time being relatively inactive, as when he returned home he would have plenty of catch-up work with his excavating business.

Just at noon one day the State Trooper super cub landed. I walked down to invite the game warden up for a coffee. He had his bear sealing equipment along so the hide and skull were documented and made ready for shipment to Seattle, avoiding having to get all that done in Kotzebue before departure.

Much too soon we bid Jason good-bye at the Kotzebue airport. His return had been fulfilling for us all.

Chapter Fourteen
Reno's Caribou

The 2016 season was a bust for most Guides and Transporters in NW Alaska after the Federal Subsistence Board closed caribou hunting to all but local subsistence users. The closure was an abuse of power by primarily the chairman of the board, but, over objections from other members, it was allowed to stand for that year.

That closure was a horrible precedent for all non-subsistence hunting in Alaska. In hopes of bringing reason to the table regarding caribou seasons and harvest limits, I along with other members of the Alaska Professional Hunters' Association, as well as resident hunters spent a lot of time in phone conferences and meetings, as well as dollars on travel. First we tried to avoid the closure, then we worked to open future years.

Finally, in mid summer, 2017, I got word that caribou hunting was restored for residents, non-resident and alien hunters for the fall season. The limit for most people would be one caribou per year, but for local subsistence hunters it would be five caribou per day. We had only the month of July to book hunters for the coming August and September.

On the morning of April 25, 2017 I received a call from a fellow named Reno, who lived in Arkansas. We had a long visit during which I learned that Reno lived in Yell County - the home of little Mattie from TRUE GRIT - one of my favorite movies. Reno's first interest was in caribou. I told him that I believed the closure would be lifted in my areas, but such action had not been officially announced.

I've never liked a hard sell and have always avoided being too persistent - or pestiferous - with any prospective hunting guests. Over two months passed before I sent Reno a short email message asking if he was still thinking of hunting with us in northwest arctic Alaska, adding that, for sure, caribou would be legal to hunt in 2017.

He replied that he was very interested in coming and that he and his wife were in Soldotna, Alaska for the summer, to do some fishing.

With so little time to book fall hunters, I offered Reno a reduced daily rate. Something I seldom do. At that rate, if he did not collect a trophy caribou, I would be running several hundred dollars in the red. But even at reduced rates, some guests are better than none at all.

After I booked Reno and received his deposit, he sent an email explaining that he suffered from sleep apnea and asked if my solar panel and battery system would be able to handle the breathing device which he used every night.

Immediately I told Reno that my system was small and I would not know if it was even functioning until I arrived with him and Ron at the lodge.

But Reno was set on hunting caribou and told me that he had ordered a solar panel and was having it shipped to the charter outfit I used - Eric Sieh's Arctic Back Country Flying. He said he was looking for a large battery to send up along with the solar panel. He planned to leave the entire system at the lodge when he departed.

Yes, this man was determined to hunt caribou.

I departed Kodiak on Monday, August 28. Ron and I met at the Anchorage airport. As connections from Kodiak to Kotzebue always include a long layover in Anchorage I had scheduled a book signing at the Mosquito Books store at the airport. Ron and I got to Kotzebue at six that evening.

My long time friends Mike, Jerry, and Chuck, and a friend of Chuck's, named Ron, were in Kotzebue with three super cubs and planning to stop by the lodge so I sent Ron and as much freight as I could stuff into their aircraft that evening. I sent the satellite telephone up with Ron who, upon arrival, reported everything in good condition, but the country was dry, with low water levels in the creeks and few berries, however there were many caribou all around the lodge. This news fueled my hope that Reno would get an opportunity to take a super nice bull. Certainly no previous hunter had exerted such extraordinary interest and effort to hunt caribou with me.

Reno arrived in Kotzebue as scheduled at eleven the next morning. I had not met Reno, nor had I seen a photograph of him, but when I saw a fellow of about my age in faded bib overalls deplane the Alaska Airlines jet, I knew it must be our guest from Yell County, Arkansas.

We were due to go the the lodge on a Cessna 206 charter the next morning, but a strong northeast wind was blowing far to the east of us, which led the pilot to delay our trip until late afternoon. A northeast blow is known as the "widow-maker" wind in northwest Alaska. But, as Ron had not called mentioning adverse conditions, as he would have done if the wind was too severe, I told the pilot we should just go. So we departed with the pilot telling me if we had to turn back, it would be at my expense. The trip was uneventful. We arrived to find a light wind. thirty-four degrees, scattered snow showers north of us, and hundreds of caribou at Trail Creek.

After introductions all around, Ron and Reno easily set up the solar panel and battery to run his night breathing device - a CPAP machine. Sighting in Reno's rifle was next.

I took a quick walk around the buildings, noting that no woodpecker holes had been bored into the siding since the previous summer. As usual grizzly bear hair seemed to grow from all the corners of the buildings, indicating where the bruins had worked at satisfying an itch. A couple of new mud wallows had been dug near the shop building, but the place seemed to have overwintered well.

Jerry had taken one bull with his bow, so we dined on fresh caribou backstrap for supper. I had encouraged them all to take as many caribou as they could, as I would be happy to put the meat in my freezer to share with Ron, however the one bull was all they put on the ground. My friends had originally planned to stay with us at the lodge for a day or so, but weather considerations caused them to change their plans by returning to Kotzebue the next day with the meat of the caribou. They planned to fuel up their cubs and fly the arctic coast from Kotzebue to the Canadian border.

A bit after eleven the next morning the three super cubs departed. Mike said he might return and spend the time with us rather than fly the coast. I hoped he would to that for visiting as well as to harvest more caribou meat, (Ron and I cannot harvest meat for ourselves while we have a contracted hunter in our company) but Mike opted to follow the other aircraft out of Kotzebue.

Being concerned about Reno's breathing, I suggested he stay upstairs, to be close enough that Ron and I could monitor his breathing, but he preferred to stay in a first floor guest room. We checked on him several times each night.

We saw caribou every day, throughout the daylight hours, but the numbers dropped from hundreds to dozens of new animals by the end of the week.

On Friday, September 1, the Alaska Department of Fish and Game protection officer stationed in Kotzebue stopped by. As always I asked him to check our paperwork, rather than wait for him to ask to do so. All was in order and we enjoyed a cup of coffee before he departed to check Transported camps in that part of Game Management Unit 23.

The next couple of days were pretty slow with a few dozen caribou moving down the valley, but we saw no big bulls. I dug a new outhouse hole, Ron and I placed a new piece of tarpaper on a section of the shop roof.

Ron and Reno hiked up the creek observing signs of bears and wolves as they evaluated the few caribou they saw each day.

On September 5 as we finished a bacon and eggs breakfast I spotted ten bull caribou on the northwest fan. All but three of these bulls were clearly takers, but one appeared just a shade better than the rest. Closer scrutiny with the 15 to 60 power spotting scope confirmed what my binoculars had revealed. I believed that band of caribou might include the top three animals taken in the entire state. They were that good!

The caribou all laid out in a sunny patch of tundra. We got ready to go, but held back to see if the animals would move.

And move they did! For no discernible reason the whole bunch of bulls stood up and began a steady march down stream. Their movements seemed casual, but they were covering country much faster than a man could walk - or trot. I decided to remain at the windows as Ron and Reno headed due west to hopefully intercept the rapidly traveling band of bulls.

The three animals in front turned up the slope to the top of the moguls at the mouth of West Bowl Creek. I expected them to go on into the canyon as I have seen happen so often, but instead they meandered around for a good half hour before one found a route through the rocks, which put them back on the west alluvial fan and again headed down creek at a rapid pace.

Reno's Caribou

Ron had seen the band begin their descent from the top of the moguls and had taken Reno across Trail Creek to a cut bank of the west fan. He did not see the caribou cross through the cottonwoods on West Bowl Creek, but he anticipated their move and saw the tops of their antlers as they wound their way through the waist high pucker brush on the south side of the creek. I hoisted a signal flag on the downstream side fo the lodge.

This did not bode well for Reno getting a shot, as he could only see the tops of the antlers and they were over two hundred yards from his position.

But sometimes it seems that old Murphy naps. The biggest bull followed two others up a scree slope while the rest of the animals continued through the brush. Reno had one chance for a snap shot as the bulls continued their rapid pace. His aim was practiced and accurate and the best bull of the bunch dropped from a neck shot.

From my window position I was not aware of the three animals going up the scree slope, nor did I hear the shot.

To my great chagrin I saw the band of bulls alternately walking and trotting through the boulders and brush south of West Bowl Creek. I felt like we had been robbed!

As the caribou moved ever further away I was able to count only nine animals. Furthermore, the one I had selected as the best did not appear to be in that number. Could it be? Now I began to think that maybe Reno had taken that truly fine bull.

The caribou had soon passed out of sight, so I busied myself with cutting wood for the sauna and gathering up what would become our dinner. After a bit less than an hour I went again to the window and saw Reno walking up the runway.

When he came to the lodge I asked him to show me his hands, but I detected no blood as he had washed in the creek. Reno knew what I was doing and told me not to worry, the big one was in the bag.

I suggested that Reno take off his boots and relax while I went to help Ron get the meat and rack back to the lodge. Reno did not want to have a shoulder mount done, so that made less work for us.

The photos do not accurately reveal the truly outstanding antler development this bull showed. His bez points had many lengthy projections and

Reno and his dandy bull.

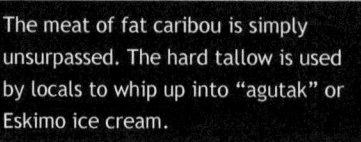
The meat of fat caribou is simply unsurpassed. The hard tallow is used by locals to whip up into "agutak" or Eskimo ice cream.

The APHA/SCI Awards are nice.

the top points and back points were exceptionally long. The rack was very well balanced.

Reno said he led the animal a bit and that resulted in a neck and head shot, so none of the wonderful meat was lost.

I scored the head the next day. It totaled a bit under the magical 400, but I felt it had a good chance to place in the top three of the Alaska Professional Hunters' Association/ Safari Club International Annual "Big 3 Competition."

Recent rule changes made it necessary for Reno to have someone other than his guide score the rack, so he had it done in Arkansas. Caribou are one of the most complex and difficult big game animals to score and I find many errors in sheets done in the "South 48" that I have reviewed. I was not happy with the measurement Reno got, but that's what I used to enter his trophy in the contest. In December, 2018 we learned that, in spite of an erroneous lower score, his bull placed number one in the competition!

The evening after Reno's big Caribou fell to his one shot, a lone bull muskox appeared to be grazing off the end of the runway just before dark. We three headed toward the animal to take some photographs, but the light faded too fast for us. I hoped, actually expected, to see the animal early the next morning, but we found only his ambling tracks as he wandered up the valley.

As we walked around hoping to sight the muskox, it became clear that the Caribou annual post-calving aggregational movement which normally occurs with a large number of animals moving up Trail Creek between July 5 and July 15 did occur in 2017. The fresh deeply rutted and muddy trails left evidence of the passage of thousands of the tundra deer. Tracks indicated that since July caribou had been wandering up and down Trail Creek on a daily basis. By mid-August most of the tracks led downstream.

We had enjoyed wonderful warm, nearly windless weather, but we may have overdrawn on our good weather account, as it began to rain and blow. When we arrived on Aug.30, our nearest creek, the Dipwater branch was dry - this is not usually the case in August. The tundra showed signs of it having been an abnormally dry season on Trail Creek - which was contrary to the rainfall reports for NW Alaska at large. By September 9, it seemed the rain was trying to live up to its expected annual performance.

ALASKA CARIBOU

Our next group of three hunting guests were from near Orlando, Florida. The hurricanes Harvey, Irma and Maria were of great concern to the folks from Florida. One of our guests was the mayor of Orlando. He felt obligated to remain in his battered city. None of the three guests made it to Kotzebue in time to catch the charter flight to Trail Creek which would take Reno back to civilization on September 10. Ron and I were surprised to see the Cessna 206 land with no one but the pilot aboard.

I was finally able to reach the organizer of the hunting group with my satellite phone. He told me that the hunters would try to arrive as soon as possible, but they could not give a date.

So Reno saw the best of our fall season and took the best caribou from Alaska home to Yell County with him. Occasionally things do turn out the way they should.

Chapter Fifteen
A Night on Heated Gravel

In the 1970s it was legal to take Caribou and most any other big game animal, except Dall rams and Brown/Grizzly bears in Alaska on the same day the hunter was airborne.

The general public opinion was that people in airplanes would swoop in on animals, jump out and shoot the terrified, running animals. That was rarely the case, but in the influential court of public opinion, aircraft using hunters were all judged guilty.

In 1974 a single Caribou hunter arrived in Kotzebue. He had called from Anchorage. I had time and told him to come on up, without asking much about him, such as his physical condition, weight, etc. I was shocked to see this grossly overweight fellow. I might not have agreed to take him, had I known his weight and condition. Thereafter inquiring about those aspects of a prospective guest became part of my pre-booking routine. One must grow and modify one's procedures with experience. And one must avoid making presumptions about strangers.

His name was Lester and he said he went by the name Les. I wished he was less, for sure. In cases like this, less would be more.

This fellow was very pleasant in manner and I wanted to see him be successful in his quest for a caribou. However it was early August and the caribou were scattered mostly over the North Slope.

I picked the man up at the Wien Air Alaska terminal, took him to my home to allow him to change clothes and leave his hard gun case. My wife and I fed him some coffee and fresh homemade doughnuts. Then we were off to the airplane.

Getting this large individual into the back seat of the Super Cub was a challenge. I used an milk crate next to the aircraft for him to stand on, then

I had him launch his derriere over the side of the cub and into the rear seat. The front seat of the cub was in full forward position and with patience over-riding my frustration, I assisted him in getting first his left leg, then his right leg into the back. It was time consuming and wrenchingly uncomfortable for both of us. I borrowed a seat belt extension from Leon Shellabarger in order for my standard belt to fit around his more than ample middle. I placed the milk crate behind the passenger for use in unloading my circus sized human life form.

With the additional problems due to his girth and weight, I decided to leave my labrador, Zeke, in town. Zeke pleaded and whined.

The trip to the cabin was uneventful and the fellow seemed to really enjoy the experience. I gave a running commentary as we flew over frost polygons in various shapes and sizes, pingos, lakes, mountains, Dall sheep, moose and grizzly bears.

We landed at our original little twelve foot by twelve foot cabin. Extracting this obese man was almost as difficult as loading him. With the milk crate again beneath the side of the plane, I managed to get his legs outside the cabin with his butt still on the seat. Then I had him embrace me around my neck and together we hoisted his bulk out of the cub. This maneuver consumed more than twenty minutes, during which he did not complain. For that he earned my admiration. However we both grunted a lot. It must have been extremely uncomfortable for him - maybe even more so than for me. I was impressed that he did not complain -ever. Handling moose quarters would never again seem like a big chore to me.

Several times I cautioned Les to use only the overhead metal tubes and the back of my seat for pulling himself and to avoid gripping the fabric side of the airplane as pressure would result in damage.

Les had a pair of knee-high rubber boots as well as a pair of hipboots. With the creeks high I needed to help him into his hipboots, which took more than twenty minutes of constant mutual struggling and grunting. I secretly wondered what manner of critter our grunts might call in for us.

The little cabin was small, but it was cozy and had two beds. The wife and dog were not with us. Best of all, we'd flown over several grizzlies and the shelter offered solid wall security between us and the wilds outside.

A Night on Heated Gravel

Less complimented the accommodations. He was dreading having to sleep in a tent.

Les and I slept well after a supper of moose steaks and spuds. He had thought to bring a bottle of good bourbon, which we both enjoyed. The tiny shelter was cozy and gave one a sense of security.

With only around four hours of semi-darkness, we awakened about seven the next morning. I went out to pee, then got on the roof to glass the valley for animals. Seeing nothing of interest I went about making a pot of coffee, then cooking up some bacon and eggs. Less offered to do the dishes, so I went about preparing the outhouse. Bears always destroy the simple frame I used, but tacking it back together and putting the tarp in place took only a half hour.

Les was just too big and otherwise compromised to let him get on the roof, which would have been a danger to him and the roof. After breakfast we crossed the small bog and found a good place to sit and glass on the east side of the cabin. He did not walk well, carrying so much extra weight as he was. We traveled only about five hundred yards from the cabin. I was concerned that he might over stress his knees or ankles.

Depending on insect harassment and other factors, a herd may travel thirty-five miles or more in a single day. Often abandoned calves or sometimes adult animals will stray from the herd and remain in the valley. Most calves are soon found and devoured by wolves or grizzly bears, while the bulls spend the summer growing antlers and making meat. I was hoping

Normally large herds of caribou come up or down Trail Creek between July 5 and July 15 - which was three weeks prior to our arrival. Trails were evident, giving the appearance that a large army had passed.

for some to show up for Les, but after three days of glassing, we saw only five grizzly bears, many Dall sheep, and three moose, but no caribou.

Les had a week to hunt and he remained enthusiastic and entertained by whatever we found. I liked the guy. One afternoon on the hills close to the cabin we found a small grasshopper. I had seen those little insects up in sheep country, but I had never before found one so low in the valley. Les joked that he might want to capture one to take home.

Day four arrived with clear skies and little wind. I decided to take Les to the North Slope where I figured most of the caribou must be. I'd left town with full tanks giving me four and a half hours flying time. With my circus-sized guest, I decided to not add fuel. Three hours of fuel would be safe enough.

So again, loading my guest into the cramped back seat of the cub was a full half hour struggle for both of us. I planned to weigh this behemoth when we got back to town - maybe at the airport luggage scale. I was certain he would tip the scales at well over three hundred pounds.

In 1986 I had a true physical Ubermensch, named Willie Benzko who was nearly seven feet tall and weighed over three hundred pounds. But this super man was pure bone and muscle, with no fat to be found on him. And he could pretty well load himself into the back of the cub, then remain pretzeled in place for hours if necessary.

So we loaded up with some lunch fixin's and little else, then departed about mid-morning. I expected to find a place to land near enough to some decent caribou, harvest one and return to the cabin that afternoon. With

A Night on Heated Gravel

My six feet two inches appear to be dwarfed by my friend Willie Benzko.

Not more than thirty minutes after take off we came onto a large herd in the mountains just north of the summit of the Brooks Range.

so much weight already behind me, I would need to tie the meat, along with the antlers on the wing struts.

That really got Les excited. He had never before seen so many wild animals in one bunch. He said it reminded him of pictures he'd seen of herds of wildebeest in Africa. But I had to find a band of bulls we could access. I followed the Utukok River as it drained to the north.

Downstream about twenty miles I found what I was looking for. A solid column of caribou was crossing a branch of the river. Fresh, muddy trails indicated this band was following where another had recently passed and more were coming. I flew back to the east and saw caribou for more than five miles, all headed toward the crossing on the Utukok.

It seems caribou mindlessly follow the trails of others.

I picked out a good looking gravel bar about a quarter of a mile from the crossing shown above. I'd burned off about one hundred pounds of fuel, but still, I needed more room than normal to land with my heavy load.

And I was anticipating to add another hundred and twenty pounds of caribou before we took off.

The wind was about twelve miles per hour and permitted a landing straight into the wind. I needed no breaks to get stopped on this fine, firm natural runway.

Les was really excited, so I urged him to take everything slow to avoid mishap. The last thing I wanted was for him to sprain an ankle.

We carefully made our way toward the crossing using what little vegetation there was to conceal our approach. We spent almost an hour picking our way to a spot that would put us behind some brush within a hundred yards of the crossing.

But the living string of caribou was petering out. I reminded Les that there were several miles of caribou coming our way and we must be patient.

A thin line of stragglers came to within fifty yards of our position. Les wanted to shoot one, but I urged him to hold out for a better rack.

There were only two to three year old bulls, and all "rag horns." We surely could do better. So Les held his fire.

These youngsters are confused, but dutifully following the trail.

We ate our sandwiches and remained in the same spot for nearly four hours. Then the caribou quit coming.

We were getting chilly. I dreaded going back to the cabin, only to have to load Les up and return the next day. I had sleeping bags in the front and rear seats, but Les would not fit into either. No matter how warm the day has been, at night a person sleeping on the ground in the far north will get uncomfortably cold. I left Les in our concealed spot, cautioning him to not shoot unless he saw a really outstanding set of antlers, or a wolf.

I tied the airplane to the scrub willows for the night, then I began to dig a trench wide enough for me and my guest. I kept the sand and gravel near for imminent use. It took some scrounging to gather enough dead wood to line the pit with the branches. I got the wood burning and kept adding whatever combustibles I could find. The spring flood had produced piles of small sticks here and there which I was happy to use. The wood was old and willow does not make a good fire anyway - it burns too fast - almost like paper, but there was no smoke. After an hour of tending and adding sticks to the fire I returned to Les.

When I went to retrieve Les he was shivering. Our short walk back to the airplane warmed him up, but he wondered how we would make it through the night with no tent. It was past nine o'clock in the evening. I began to shovel the sand and gravel back over the smoldering wood. I piled at least four inches of sand and gravel on top of the hot coals.

We sat on the heated sand and gravel to wolf down our light supper before lying down on our warmed beds. I placed space blankets on the ground for us to lie on, then I unzipped the sleeping bags and we used them like a blanket. And that is how we spent the next seven hours. I slept reasonably well and did not feel cold. Les said he had done okay. Without our heated beds, we would both have suffered an uncomfortably cold night.

I had a small thermos of coffee and a package of store-bought Bear Claw pastries and some fried meat my wife had sent with us, which we finished just as another large group of caribou came our way. They came on a slow run, so close we could hear their hooves clicking. Les asked me about the clicks and I told him that I had read that their Tendons snap over sesamoid bones in their feet, and that's what makes the click. Experts think the clicking helps the members of a herd stay in contact, especially in snowstorms or, say, when it's foggy.

Many caribou passed close to the tied airplane. A few startled, but most just glanced at it and moved along. Less was still sitting on his overnight bed of coals when I spotted a better than average bull and told him to get ready.

With the decent bull not more than thirty yards from us, Les shot it in the neck and it went down immediately.

Both Les and I were pleased. As I skinned and butchered the animal, the breeze picked up again from the north which would allow me to take off directly into the wind.

I tied the antlers and front shoulders on the left wing strut with the hind quarters and ribs on the right. I placed the tenderloins and backstraps in a plastic bag which I had Les hold in his lap.

For his third loading into the cub, Les was more confident and experienced and it may have taken less than a half hour.

On our hour long flight back to the cabin we saw thousands of caribou, one pack of five wolves and half a dozen grizzly bears.

We spent one more night in the cabin, enjoyed bourbon libations, had a breakfast of tenderloins, eggs and toast, and were headed back to Kotzebue shortly after noon.

Considering the time of year, the limited mobility of my guest and other considerations, this was an acceptable, symmetrical bull. The hide was absolutely beautiful!

Having flown three of the four and a half hours of full fuel tanks, I added ten gallons of 80/87 gasoline to give us ample margin of extra flying time if needed.

Less spent the evening with my family and me. He said he had enjoyed the most wonderful hunting experience of his life. After a fine supper prepared by my wife Mae, he said he wanted to be up front with me. He was going to have to renege on the agreed price of the trip. I had agreed to take him for twelve hundred dollars. He doubled the fee for the fine job!

At the airport the next morning I got Les to step on the luggage scale and it indicated he weighed 365 pounds. He said he might have lost a little on the trip!

Chapter Sixteen
Franco and the Montanans

In the fall of 1985 I had booked a man and wife from Montana for the same period that Francisco Franco from Spain would be with us.

I had known the man, whom I will call Cal, for many years, but I had not met his new wife. Very soon I saw that Dee could cook, clean, and shoot. She volunteered and did them all very well.

They came in on the late afternoon Alaska Airlines flight and luckily all their baggage arrived at the same time. We drove the one block to my house and spent an enjoyable evening over my spaghetti preparation and store-bought apple pie. They loved my Labrador, Max and he loved most people. We focused our discussion on the three species he wanted to collect which were caribou, a Dall ram and a grizzly.

Cal was what many folks refer to as a hunting fool. He lived and breathed hunting anything from ring-necked pheasants to whatever big game animal was available. He talked hunting continuously, even, I was told, while attending a church service.

Oh well, I can think of many worse afflictions. It was challenging to steer the conversation toward subjects other than what I expected to take place that day or week at the lodge. I tried to tell him that I could accurately relate past events but I had no crystal ball for telling the future. However, as I had been conducting hunts in essentially the same way and from the same location for almost twenty years, it is reasonable to expect similar events for the coming two weeks.

In between Cal's questions, all of which were nothing more than slight variations of the previous ones, I did learn a little about his new wife. Dee was Montana born and raised and had always enjoyed hunting, fishing and other outdoor activities. She seemed an ideal match for Cal. One of her hobbies had turned into a part time vocation. That was sculpture. She crafted her figures in wax or clay, then took them to a casting facility for transformation into bronze. That went well with an outdoorsy lifestyle. She had talent and loved wilderness and wild animals.

The following morning my guest from Spain, Francis Franco arrived in company with one body guard. This man was the biological grandson of Generalissimo Franco, but lacking a male heir to perpetuate his great wealth, the Generalissimo adopted his first born grandson - Francis.

The previous January I had met Senor Franco in person while I was in Spain and we had drafted and signed a hunting contract for the pursuit of a Dall ram and a bull moose. But the agreement did not include any other guests. My fee for non-hunting companions was $300 per day at the time. Bookings were for 10 days minimum. Francis arrived accompanied by a bodyguard. The additional person would necessitate either two extra charters or two extra three hour round trips in my super cub. I explained this to Francis Franco to which he replied that I would receive so many guests after using him as a reference, he should not have to pay for his body guard.

This over indulged Spaniard was accustomed to having his every demand met without question - I had seen that while in his company in Spain, but I would not acquiesce to allowing him to dictate new terms or to pay less than the going rate. I felt anger building within me. My face flushed red.

Seeing my reaction, Franco offered to give me a check to cover the charges for his body guard, but I did not trust him and I insisted that he have his bank make a wire transfer to my bank. I would take the Montana couple and the body guard to the lodge and return for him later in the afternoon. That should allow enough time for the fund transfer. My son, Martin, would serve as bodyguard of my house and my possessions, more than Franco, in my absence. I told Martin to monitor Franco closely and to get time and charges on any telephone calls he made from my number.

So, off we went. I chartered a Cessna 170 to take the Montana folks and I put the body guard, Rolando, in the back of my cub with my dog, Max, on his lap. I speak Spanish reasonably well, so that made a comfortable experience for us both.

I had departed twenty minutes earlier than the other aircraft and arrived at Trail Creek ahead of him. The valley was peppered with caribou. I

A massive movement of Barren Ground Caribou near the lodge.

Caribou between the lodge and the runway.

estimated that there were more than four thousand within two miles fo the lodge. Rolando and I were carrying gear and food to the lodge when the Cessna landed. As soon as the pilot stopped the engine, caribou drifted right back onto the runway.

Cal was in a high state of excitement. Immediately he filled his rifle magazine and volunteered to shot a caribou for camp meat. I told him that we could not take any big game animals until after 2:00 am of the morning after the flight and that every animal taken must be tagged. Additionally, our trophy animals would serve quite nicely as camp meat. Cal remained in a state of high twitch. I asked Dee to watch over Max and to be sure he stayed close to her while I went back for Franco. I should have told her to keep Cal legal.

After getting all the stuff to the lodge and showing everyone where the outhouse would be when I returned and had time to get it set up, where they should dip water, etc., I returned to Kotzebue to see if Franco had made the bank transfer. I did not want to burden Martin with this difficult guest any longer than absolutely necessary.

My bank verified that the transfer was in progress, but it may take a few days to complete. I figured that was as good as we would get so I fueled the cub and we headed back north.

Franco seemed to enjoy the ninety minute flight as we were seeing plenty of game, mostly caribou, but also a dozen moose, some Dall sheep and several grizzly bears.

When I landed, Cal came striding proudly to me and announced that he had shot, but not recovered a meat bull for us. He lost the blood trail in the tundra.

Damn! I know my face flushed red - I could feel it!

I reminded Cal that I told him not to do that, it was an illegal kill and by law I was expected to turn him in to the game warden. Cal's demeanor morphed from one of ecstasy to grim dread.

As I was trying to cool off, I unloaded the aircraft and noticed the Franco seemed to be enjoying the stressful situation.

I told Cal to go immediately to the lodge and bring back his caribou metal locking tag, as we would have to find the small bull and it would have to be tagged. The annual limit for non-residents was five caribou and I had more tags to sell him, but Cal was not happy to have to spend three hundred and twenty-five dollars on the tag for such a small animal.

After Cal's departure, Rolando told me in Spanish that Cal had become excited when the young bull came walking up the runway and had the impression that it was a trophy animal. Only after he shot it did Cal refer to it as camp meat. This sort of thing often happens with whitetail and mule deer hunters unaccustomed to seeing caribou racks.

With my fine dog, Max, I took Cal in search of the crippled animal, but we found no trace. I had never lost a wounded caribou and I told him that we would make its pursuit the first order of business for the following day.

If either a state or a federal game warden had visited us that day, Cal would have been in some trouble. However visits by officials were not common in our remote location, which is way back of the beyond, and we saw no one.

I wrestled with the situation, but eventually I decided to not make an uncomfortable situation worse by ending Cal's hunt. Hopefully he would calm down and follow instructions. The state would get the money from another tag and, once found, the meat would not be wasted.

This day was a prime example of why regulations require that for many big game animals, non-residents must be guided.

After a meal of baked salmon with macaroni and cheese, salad and pudding, our little group of five toasted the wilderness, the caribou and our great good fortune in sharing it all.

Making the journey from town to the lodge is always tiring. Away from everyday noises of automobiles, trains, and other common city disturbances, everyone sleeps well. The temperature normally drops to the high thirties that time of year, with occasional overnight freezing, making a good sleeping bag a delightful comfort.

The next morning my guests were up and refreshed. The magic of fresh, hot coffee had the group in fine spirits. I fried up a bunch of bacon, then started in on eggs. I broke a hen's egg over Max's dog food for a treat. My guests were all diligently glassing the hills from the windows. They found caribou everywhere.

On one of the moguls just east of the lodge stood a small bull caribou with its head down and blood stain on its left front leg. I assumed it was Cal's critter. We dispatched the animal and brought the meat to the lodge, after Cal snapped his tag on it. It took less than an hour to have it hanging on the meat rack.

A week before I had seen several legal Dall rams about four miles north of the lodge, so after breakfast I looked the area over with the spotting scope. I saw white dots where I expected the sheep to be, so we packed lunches from canned ham and headed up stream. This was his first hunt of the fall and my dog Max was super excited.

We reached the first glassing point at Current Creek and sat for an hour, but saw only caribou, lots of caribou. Franco announced that he was not at all interested in shooting any reindeer. I had already learned that most European guests equated our caribou with domestic reindeer and held our tundra deer somewhat in disdain.

As we progressed up the valley, Cal was becoming increasingly obsessed with the many opportunities we had to harvest caribou. His left index finger had a definite itch. I tried to reassure him that we had not yet seen a really super head, but when we did, we would do our best to take it. I told him that we had enough time and with so many animals we should pick and choose carefully.

As we walked up the valley I kept the Dall sheep in view before they disappeared beyond the hill. To keep them in sight we had to walk another mile toward Sea Gull Pass. When we again had a clear view of the seven sheep, only two were rams and both were sub-legal.

On the return leg of our trip, Max and I climbed a hill to peer into the Current Creek drainage. About a mile up the canyon I saw three good rams bedded on a rocky spine from which I did not see any approach but from below. I planned to make a try for them the next day.

As so commonly happens, this jaunt turned out to be much longer than originally anticipated and before we reached the lodge, Rolando, Francis and Cal were physically squeezed out and showing signs of irritability. I, too, was relieved to not have to walk another mile. But Dee was as bouncy and full of energy after our eight hours in the field as she was at breakfast time. All of her hundred and ten pounds or so, was pure dynamic energy and enthusiasm.

The next morning, Cal who was ten years my senior, was stiff and sore. Rolando asked for aspirin for his aches, but Dee, Francis and I had recovered painlessly from the journey.

As we sipped the first cup of coffee I mentioned that we should get after those rams right away, and hope to find them in the same place, as they may move into a nearby and much more difficult location at any time. Cal said he was not going to make the trip. He was convinced that like the day before, we would find the rams to be too small to take.

I did not try to talk Cal into coming, other than to tell him that these were all better than just the legal full curl. The promontory that the rams were bedded would be difficult to approach and could only be made by

Part of a band of big bull caribou a quarter of a mile from the lodge.

following the bottom of the valley before ascending the spine occupied by the rams. When Rolando mentioned he would remain in the lodge, I did not try to change his mind either. Having a single shooter with me improved our chances of approaching the rams.

As I was walking down the stairs Dee asked if she could use a bag of fresh picked wild blueberries for a pie. She had seen the ziplock bag in our cool box. I told her a pie would be wonderful.

The week before I had taken my son, Martin on a scouting trip on which he had shot a large black bear. The bear had been gorging on blue berries, so its meat would be delicious. The stomach was packed full of partially chewed berries, so I tied a string around each end of the stomach and took it home. Picking those several pounds of berries would have required more time than we had to spare. I had harvested bear-picked berries before. When we arrived home, I emptied the stomach contents into a gallon zip lock bag and placed it in the refrigerator. That was the bag Dee found in our cool box.

Francis and I had only a twenty minute walk to the mouth of Current Creek, but Murphy was with us. We walked right into a band of caribou bulls which included a couple of takers. They carried the best racks that I had seen so far this season.

When we reached the top of the hill separating Current Creek from the main valley I was pleased to see the trio of rams bedded in nearly the same spots they used the afternoon before. But, as is so often the case with sheep, they were lying with heads up and directed down the drainage, through which we had to make our way unseen. We backed off the hill and started up the creek completely out of sight of the sheep. In places we had no choice but to expose ourselves to the rams, we proceeded very slowly and were not detected by our quarry. It took ninety minutes to reach the base of the rocky spine upon which the rams were resting.

The spine was steep, making most of our ascent out of sight of the rams, but we crept up as cautiously as burglars, avoiding dislodging any rocks. This was even slower than our trek up the creek, but in about an hour we were as close as we would ever get. I could clearly see two of the rams, but I wanted to inspect the other before having Francis settle on which I judged to be the best trophy head.

We had worked up a bit of a sweat and lying motionless on the rocks, we soon felt a chill. Our sweat had brought on a fierce attack of mosquitos as well. We could only hand crush the bugs, rather than making noise by slapping them. Sounds are amplified in the mountains. In our tense situation, it seemed like the buzzing bugs were as loud as gasoline engines.

Francis told me that either ram was acceptable to him. I urged him to be patient -to flex his muscles - even do some push-ups to get warm.

After what seemed like half of forever, one of the visible rams stood up and stretched. In so doing he dislodged a rock which went crashing down the mountain side. This brought the other rams to their feet and the third ram, now fully visible, was a bit below the others, and offered a broadside shot for my guest. The third ram looked a bit longer in both horns than his companions, however his left horn was broken and bent inward. Nevertheless, he was the best of the group, so I told Francis to shoot him.

The only redeeming virtue I had so far discovered in Francis was his above average shooting ability. His 8mm bullet impacted the ram on the left side, just behind the shoulder, a perfect hit. The ram shuddered, raised up on its hind legs and tumbled down the mountain. The companion rams watched as the carcass bounced and rolled, then they turned and calmly walked further up the spine into an outcropping of nearly impenetrable rocks.

This ram was rolling in fat and was a good representative of its species. The broken and bent horn tip could be repaired by a taxidermist if desired.

Somehow the long, cautious stalk had consumed most of the day. I quickly butchered and loaded the meat into my pack, including the long bones and ribs. Francis carried the head and cape.

The Spaniard's ram -37 ½ inches.

We were out of the side valley of Current Creek, in less than an hour and entered the lodge forty minutes after that. Sheep hunting doesn't get much better, or easier than that.

Francis was quick to tell Cal that he should have come along as the other two rams were nearly as good as his. Cal squirmed a little, but did not reply.

Yeah, as it worked out, Cal could have had his ram that day, too.

Dee had prepared a heaping plate of chicken-fried caribou back strap, mashed potatoes with gravy and a green salad.

She followed me into my bedroom and quietly asked, "Jake, who picked those berries?"

"Oh, you wouldn't know him," I replied.

She said she found some tiny teeth that looked like rodent incisors amongst the berries. She knew animal anatomy well. I told her that our Alaskan mosquitos are mighty fierce and sometimes toothy, too.

I figured the bear must have eaten a muskrat or young beaver a few hours before Martin shot it. I was certain it would not bother Dee or Cal,

Max was often at the window, watching for game.

but my Spanish guests might take offense if they knew the source of the berries in the pie. So I declined to offer more details.

The pie, by the way, was pronounced delicious by everyone.

That evening with everyone's wine glass full, I insisted on doing the dishes, though Dee argued about that, I prevailed.

I took the two buckets outside to fill at the dip water creek about eight yards from the cabin and heard caribou grunting in the willows toward the runway.

When I returned with the water buckets I noticed Max looking out the main window. We saw the tops of the racks of a dozen bull caribou on the runway. I suggested that Dee grab her rifle and come with me to look them over.

The best rack in the bunch was a dandy, with good palmation and symmetrical antlers. I asked Dee if she would like to shoot it.

It was one way of saying thank you for her wonderful work in the kitchen. Max was by my left leg and wagging his tail furiously, but he remained silent. Dee hit the caribou behind the head and he was down.

This bull was clearly worth tagging. I told Dee that I would provide a second tag for her at no cost.

Dee's caribou was the best we had seen up to that time.

Caribou bloat faster than any other animal I know, so I opened the belly and ran my knife up one side of the brisket, cut loose the diaphragm and pulled the guts out. I retrieved the heart, but we do not eat caribou liver.

We walked to the lodge, I started one three wheeler and Cal helped me load the caribou into the trailer. We hung the carcass at the meat rack and peeled the skin off. I left Cal at that chore while Max and I returned to the gut pile and drug it to a spot clearly visible from the main lodge window. Cal wanted a grizzly and wolves were open to anyone - with a twenty wolf per year limit. I saw fresh wolf tracks everyday, so there was a better than reasonable chance we might get a shot at one. And I had seen several grizzlies on the flight with Francis.

It rained for an hour or two that night with scattered showers lingering in the morning. Everyone awoke refreshed and cheerful. The rain had brought out some delightful tundra smells, most noticeably that of the very aromatic Labrador Tea. Fresh brewed coffee soon added to the morning's glory.

A large willow patch on the east side of Trail Creek and about a mile and a half downstream from the lodge often held moose as they moved up and down the valley in September. We had not yet scrutinized that area, but it was a good bet for the day. Our group of five crossed East Bowl Creek and leisurely sidehilled down the valley. From the our position just north of the South Overlook I noticed some dark forms in the brush that could only be moose.

We found comfortable, dry hummocks to sit and study the willows below and about a quarter of a mile from us. I caught the outstanding white of antlers freshly shed of velvet on two animals, so we had at least two large bulls in the brush. I wanted to evaluate the racks and see all the moose. Cal whispered that now he, too, would like to take a moose. I told him we would only take one moose today and we needed to pay attention to how we went about it. We had a relatively long trek to pack out the meat. Bull moose weigh around sixteen hundred pounds of which about one thousand pounds must be carried from the kill site for consumption. If a shoulder mount is planned, add another eighty-five pounds. I figured a minimum of eight maximum man loads (stagger loads) per moose. So if one of the bulls is a taker, we need to plan the stalk and the eventual kill to avoid a spooked or a wounded animal running further down the creek. Every step the moose took would require that we take eight steps recovering the meat and trophy.

A light breeze developed and was blowing up the creek - from the moose to us. We sat above and directly cross wind to the moose. There was virtually no chance of the animals smelling us.

After more than an hour of careful glassing I had discovered a third bull and decided on which was clearly the largest trophy. The same willow thicket, which was more than a mile in length, held at least four mature cow moose. We must avoid alarming the cows as they are more apt to spook and run than are bulls. The bulls would simply follow the cows.

So I developed a plan. I would send Dee and Cal along the hillside to the far end of the willow patch. After exactly thirty minutes they were to walk with the wind at their back and about fifty yards apart as they came back to the north through the dense willows. They did not need to make a quiet stalk. I wanted the moose to be aware of the two "drivers" and simply move up the willow patch, as they so often do when being stalked. I did not want the moose to panic, which would add unnecessary confusion to the situation and could result in the moose running downstream.

In front of everyone, I cautioned Cal to not shoot any moose, no matter what happens.

Francis, Rolando and I would move back along the hillside, tracing our route down, then turn down East Bowl Creek to watch the top end of the willow patch. We positioned ourselves on top of an ancient glacial esker of about sixty feet in height, giving us a good, elevated view of the area. When I identified the biggest bull, I would instruct Francis to shoot it.

So we sat and quietly crushed the pestiferous mosquitoes that the rain had brought out in kamikaze attacks. I had some "Deet" repellent that I shared with my guests.

After a brief wait I heard antlers passing through brush and soon I saw the first dark brown body emerging from the willows. It was a cow. The animal stopped and looked around before continuing her journey north. Another big cow and a small bull followed the steps of the lead animal. So, we had now seen only three of the seven or more moose in the area.

Walking abreast, the two big bulls appeared at the edge of the willows and stopped to look for the cows. The best bull was the one furthest from us. I told Francis to wait until the bulls crossed the small creek and to hold for an unobstructed shot. I told him to aim for the shoulder - not just behind the shoulder. I wanted a broken front leg. I expected the bull to take the shoulder shot and then follow the cows which were headed in the direction of the lodge. I preferred that the big animal drop as close to his meat's final destination as possible. The more open conditions would give Francis ample opportunity for at least one more shot.

So all went as I had hoped, but when Francis' bullet smacked the bull, the great beast wheeled around and ran back into the brush from whence he had come. The other bull did the expected thing and jogged north in the path of the cows.

Another cow, apparently alarmed by the stricken bull, came charging out of the willows and headed north to join the group. I cautioned silence and hoped our bull would soon come out and move to join the others.

We sat for less than a minute beforeI heard a shot from the willow patch. I figured Cal had seen the wounded bull and tried to shoot it. Ratz! My cheeks flushed red and angry.

In a few seconds Cal hollered that he had dropped the moose. I was not happy to hear that. Cal sounded proud of himself!

Francis, Rolando and I had less than two hundred yards to reach the scene. The stricken bull had run down stream, then, sensing the Montanan "drivers," turned back and entered Trail Creek, heading upstream. It was in midstream of a shallow branch when and where Cal dropped the big bull.

Fully expecting Francis to be upset, I was relieved when he showed no sign of anger.

Trail Creek and all its tributaries are normally clear and cold, but sand and gravel adhere to fresh meat, so in situations like this, I remove the four quarters with the hide on to help keep the meat clean and to discourage birds.

Cal asked me who would tag the moose. I told him it was Francis' animal, and too bad someone else couldn't hold their fire, as the moose was doing what I had hoped for - prior to being shot a second time - in the middle of the river, no less. I let him know I was unhappy with his action.

We got the meat laid out on freshly cut willows. I tied the six foot long back straps with neck meat attached and tenderloins on my pack board. That made about a ninety pound load. Cal volunteered to pack out the head. In those days it was legal to remove the trophy before all the meat was taken from the field.

With so many hands and two sharp knives we had the butchery completed in less than an hour. Franco did not want the cape, so I did not prepare it.

Cal and I made two more trips that day, leaving one load apiece for the morning. The morning revealed that a fox had chewed some of our meat, but there was no sign of larger carnivores. I was hoping to find a grizzly for Cal.

Francis told me that he would like to depart the next day, so after the last load of meat was hung, I loaded Rolando and as much meat as I could take in the cub and headed for Kotzebue. I took Rolando first because if my son was not available to be with whomever I took town, I preferred that Rolando make arrangements at the hotel and for the departure of himself and Francis.

The trip to town was uneventful and I had the load of meat in the freezer, the antlers on the porch, fueled the cub, and was back in three and a half hours. Then it was Francis turn to go. Of course on each trip I stuffed as much meat into the cub as I could safely haul. I would not return to the lodge until the Spaniards departed, which I hoped would be the the following morning.

Franco and the Montanans

Francis and Max on the fallen bull.

Cal and Dee cheerfully helped quarter and pack the meat.

End of the rainbow time for Franco.

Rolando had things lined up for their departure on the morning jet, so after breakfast at the hotel I got them checked in and waived them off.

The weather continued to hold beautiful. I enjoyed a tailwind to Trail Creek and flew around the valley a bit, looking for game. I saw nine Dall sheep, two of which were rams, on the near side of Popple Creek, about four miles south of the lodge. It might be a trip we could make in the next few days. I found scattered bands of caribou throughout the valley, but I could not locate a grizzly. Curiously we had seen only three grizzlies since the day we arrived and they were all at long distance. I found a total of nineteen adult moose within three miles of the lodge that morning, two of which were much larger than the one Francis took.

I arrived before noon. My two guests were finishing breakfast when I landed.

It seemed a good day to slice some moose and caribou meat for making jerky, wash some of my socks and undies and putter around doing small chores.

I checked the weather forecast with the flight service station before I departed and it looked like clear, cold conditions would prevail for another week, but after a very dark overcast night, we awoke the next morning surrounded by snow. Visibility was reduced to about a hundred yards and at times we couldn't see the sauna shed from the main lodge - a distance of fifty yards. Well, the lodge is one hundred and eighteen miles north of Kotzebue, so one can expect different weather than what is predicted.

The sauna was designed for days like this. I fired up the stove and enjoyed my sauna solo, then went in to work up a stew for supper while my guests enjoyed their ablutions.

The next day was more of the same with snow accumulating to about ten inches on the level and drifted to over three feet in places.

Caribou kept coming on their southerly route to country with a gentler winter.

We saw breaks in the overcast before sunset on the second day of snow and hoped for good conditions by morning. Time was running short for my guests and I wanted to see them take home the critters they - Cal actually - came for.

Hearing a noise, I got up about three o'clock that morning to see a clear sky punctuated by stars. There was little wind. If those conditions held, we would have a good chance of seeing grizzly tracks and following up on them.

With sandwiches of moose meat, candy bars, a jug of creek water and an apple each, we headed south to Popple Creek. It was twenty-eight degrees and despite the ice, we soon felt too warm. I removed my down vest and put it in my pack. Max was full of enthusiasm. He seemed to sense success today. The freeze-up resulted in lower water levels in all the creeks.

At the moose kill we found fresh wolf tracks and a full parliament of noisy magpies which protested our intrusion and broadcast our presence up and down the creek.

From the South Overlook I spotted Dall sheep near where I had seen some two days before, so we headed that way. We had nearly a mile of miserable pucker brush - dwarf birch that grows to nipple height on a tall man and has densely packed bases that made traversing an ankle and knee twisting nightmare. To add to that misery, there were no discernible trails through the tangled growth, The snow cover made it even more treacherous.

The sheep were feeding on a sunny slope, paying no attention to us or anything but filling their bellies.

The slippery, stumble-prone footing in the pucker brush gave way to a steep slope with loose rocks underlying the snow. We each fell numerous times, but Dee seemed to keep herself upright more than Cal or me.

I was beginning to think about how difficult it was going to be to stumble back in the dark. With a high overcast moving in from the south, it promised to be a very dark, slippery night coming.

Finally we reached a spot that seemed to be as close as we could approach the sheep. We were across a steep ravine on about the same level and about two hundred yards distant. It was time to make the shot.

The two rams could have been twins, as neither looked to be the better. The animals were separated by about fifty yards, so I told Cal to tell me which one he wanted and stay with it once the first shot was placed. He fired and the sheep did not move. He rapidly fired two more times, but the sheep only looked up hill. Cal fumbled in panic searching his pockets for more ammunition.

Dee handed him her rifle and I told Cal to take it easy. The sheep were beginning to move around, but they were not departing, so he should take it slow and squeeze carefully.

Cal and Dee with his September ram.

On the next shot, his fourth attempt, he hit the ram. The sheep shuddered and appeared shaken, but stood in place. Cal fired again and the sheep went down.

The twin ram and the other seven sheep gradually moved up the slope. Even they did not chose to run in the slippery conditions.

We hustled as fast as the conditions warranted, took some photographs, caped the ram and butchered the animal for immediate return to the comforts of the lodge. We were on our way in half an hour, with Max up front and anxious to head for home.

We slid and slipped along the side hills of the west side of Trail Creek, avoiding the bottom with its tangled pucker brush. It was a question of sixes - six of one, half a dozen of the other, regarding which was the less taxing route. Our progress was slow and exhausting due to our continual efforts to avoid a serious fall. Even Max struggled in the slippery conditions.

As expected, we drug ourselves back to the lodge well after dark. The heavy overcast had reached us and along with it came more snow. We had been granted a brief window in the weather and we'd made good use of it. Now it looked like full winter had arrived.

The cape of the ram still needed to be removed from the head, but that could wait for another day.

Cal and I hung the meat and left the head in the shop building while Dee heated up some left over moose from the previous meal. After one helping, along with a double whiskey, we were all headed for bed.

The next morning everyone, but Max, showed bruises acquired on the trip to Popple Creek.

With a cup of starting fluid - coffee - in my hand I glanced out the east window and saw a large band of caribou coming our way. This group appeared to be all large bulls. I told Dee to get downstairs and put on one of the white camouflage parkas as we were going to try to intercept that bunch.

In minutes we had crossed the now solidly frozen swamp and were using a deep glacier gut to conceal our passage to an elevated vantage spot from which we could take a caribou if we found one we wanted. Max was in his usual position, occasionally touching my right leg.

There were a dozen or more "taker" bulls in this bunch, but toward the back was a real dandy. His antlers made him unmistakable, but in addition, his coat was solid dark brown, lacking the usual white mane and gray lateral stripe.

I told Dee this was the best caribou rack I had seen all season.

We held our position, lying on our bellies in the snow as the caribou came steadily toward us. I whispered to Dee to put one up the spout, leave it on safety and hold fire until most of the animals had passed us. This should encourage them to continue on down the valley.

The leaders walked by us at only eighty yards. They were on a steady march, walking with heads low, without the usual pauses to munch on lichens as they traveled.

Only two bulls were behind the best one. It was harvest time.

Dee slipped the safety off and fired. The bull dropped straight to the ground as if pole axed. Her bullet had shattered the spinal column just inches from the back of the head.

I heard a whoop from the lodge, only three hundred yards away. Cal was pleased. Max was on his feet with tail wagging furiously.

We walked the short distance to the fallen bull and Dee gave me a genuine bear hug.

The rack shows seven points on the top part of each antler, which is usually the mark of a fully mature, trophy bull.

Dee with her second and best caribou. Max is nuzzling its belly.

Cal soon joined us. There was a debate on whether or not to have a shoulder mount made. I suggested we just cape the animal and they could decide later to use it or not.

Soon we had the trophy back at the lodge and were having a second try at coffee when the snow began, again. This was wet and heavy snow and it kept up until dark.

Conditions were clearing in the morning. My guests had reservations to catch a southbound jet the next day, so I began running the three wheeler up and down the runway to pack the snow. I used a drag weighed down with rocks to smooth it over.

That afternoon I was able to make two trips to Kotzebue with Dee and Max, then Cal and their gear. It would take two more plane loads to haul the rest of the meat, including some of Franco's moose. I could do that after their departure, if we didn't get too much more snow.

The following summer I submitted Dee's score sheet for consideration in the Alaska Professional Hunters' Association/ Safari Club International annual Big Three competition. It placed number two in the 1985 annual Big Three competition.

Chapter Seventeen
Women Who Hunt

Ladies have always been hunters, but they are represented in sport hunting far less commonly than their numbers would lead one to expect. Let the diversity and inclusion crowd agonize about that!

I favor women hunters - normally they eat less, weigh less and smell nice.

It's not infrequent that a guest brings a lady on his hunting trip. Most often the lady is just along for the trip, but many times after seeing the operation and the beautiful animals, they decide they would like to harvest one for themselves. Since caribou tags are not allotted by drawing, I can simply sell the lady a license and tag and they are legal to hunt.

Dee is pleased with her last day bull.

Two wives of guest hunters decided they wanted to collect a trophy and wound up with animals that placed in the top three of the Alaska annual Big Three Competition.

In 1985 the spouse of a Montana hunter took a caribou that placed number two in that year's competition - and it took place on the last day of her booking. Details of this guest and her trophy can be found in the previous story "Franco and the Montanans."

The wife agreed it was a great bull.
In 2008 I had booked a couple from Texas. The man wanted to take a grizzly, a caribou and as many wolves as possible. The wife had never hunted and was not planning to shoot anything.

In dealing with the guests on the booking, I spoke with the wife and the man's business associate, never with "the man." I urged the wife to be sure to have her husband read my emails and carefully review my website, better still, call me. But he was too busy to do that.

When my assistant, Ron, and I met the couple at the Kotzebue airport, the man said, "This doesn't look like Kodiak!" I said, "it doesn't look at all like Kodiak. I live in Kodiak during the winter and part of the summer, but all Arctic Rivers Guide and Booking Service big game hunts take place in the Arctic, north of Kotzebue."

It was apparent that the man had never read any of my literature or emails. Nor had anyone informed me that the wife was eight months pregnant.

I chartered a Cessna 206 to take the couple and one grandson of mine, Spencer, to the lodge. The first afternoon was spent sighting in his rifle and familiarizing the guests with the outhouse location, the sauna and how things worked in general. The fellow told me he would be pleased to take a caribou like the one hanging at the lodge. I replied that I hoped he would find an even better bull.

Day two of the booking was the man's birthday, so Ron had baked a chocolate cake and presented it just after a dinner of king crab. The wife was very appreciative, but the man seemed unimpressed.

As the cake was being cut I looked out the south window and saw a band of six caribou coming our way. Immediately one bull stood out as being worthy of close scrutiny. I put the spotting scope on it and saw amidst its blizzard of points, it had double bez and double shovels. This rack would score well over four hundred points - the gold standard for caribou racks.

I passed the scope to the hunter who announced that it was not as large as the rack in the cabin. I told him that it was at least thirty percent larger and would likely place in the top three taken in Alaska for the year. He said he just didn't think it was very big.

The wife asked to view the animal which was still coming our way. She said she liked it and would like to shoot it if her husband did not.

Quickly I filled out a non-resident hunting license and the forms for a caribou tag and in a few minutes after first seeing the animals, we were all out the door and headed toward the oncoming caribou.

The band of caribou had veered a bit west which put them in scattered willows, instead of coming up the open runway. Once our group of five people entered the willows we proceeded very slowly. The very pregnant woman was lugging along her husband's rifle, so I asked that she let me carry it for her. She handed it to me.

Within minutes I could see antlers of several bulls in the brush, and they were coming directly to us. When I located the biggest one I whispered to the woman to come forward and get ready to shoot. At that moment the husband stepped up, grabbed the rifle and fired. The range was thirty yards. The targeted bull went down and the five other bulls milled around.

The husband asked me if he had shot the right animal.

"Yes, the biggest bull is on the ground, but the wrong person shot it," I replied.

Then I asked the wife for her caribou tag and I clipped it on the fallen animal. The husband said it should be his, but he had left his tag at the lodge.

I told my grandson, Spencer, to shoot one of other large bulls. He was serving as a packer, so was legal to harvest meat for himself and as a local, his limit was fifteen caribou per day.

This is a unique rack and with double bez, unlike any I had seen before. It scored 427 ⅛ and took First Place in the annual competition.

We left Spencer and Ron to butcher the two bulls and I escorted the couple back to the lodge. There was no plan to have the outstanding animal mounted so no cape was taken.

A young girl begins to hunt.

In 1990 I met a booked hunter who had brought along his wife and daughter. It was a pleasant family and we enjoyed their company in some of the finest weather the Arctic can offer in September.

The man took an old ram with heavily groomed horns that would score number three in the statewide competition. The wife enjoyed the comforts of the lodge and the daughter was thrilled with stream fishing for Arctic Char and Grayling. She was a nice kid.

Caribou had been spotty all season. When a group of medium sized bulls appeared on the west side of the valley, the man declared that none met his standards, so he would not waste time on a stalk, but the daughter, who had little experience in shooting or hunting said that she would like to take one of the caribou. Her father agreed, so my sister, Pat, and I took the fourteen year old girl, and on her first shot at eighty yards, she decked the bull she wanted. It was not a great head, but it was a respectable representative of the species.

The young lady is pleased with her first big game animal, as Pat looks on.

As it turned out, we found no truly outstanding caribou during their booking, so it was a good thing this animal was harvested.

Beginning in 1978 with a trip to Southern Rhodesia, I made several trips to Africa.

On one of those trips I met the chief taxidermist of the Transvaal Museum. Katerina Hecker was an excellent taxidermist with a long family history which originated in Germany, moved to German East Africa or Tanzania (formerly Tanganyika), then due to Mau-Mau terrorism to Kenya, and finally to South Africa. She expressed a desire to someday visit and hunt in Alaska.

A good friend of mine, Bill Gasaway, was the chief moose biologist for the State of Alaska and knew Katerina and her family quite well. I suggested that he come up to the lodge and help with the guiding season, as he had done once before. He was a great moose caller. He was welcome to invite Katerina to hunt as well.

Snow came early and heavy that fall which resulted in a large southward movement of caribou much earlier than usual.

By mid-September the equinoctial storms kept us cabin-bound for several days. Finally the wind seemed to tire and the sky cleared. The solid snow cover made sighting animals much easier than one finds in other conditions and on the afternoon of the first clear, nearly windless day, a gang of several hundred caribou came our way.

We had only to walk across the bog and position ourselves in one of the glacial trenches until the animals came within easy shooting range.

We found no bulls with great antler formation in all components, but one had tremendous bez and shovels. Katerina liked that one and with one shot she anchored it. If only the upper antler development had matched the lower. But, still, it was a a worthy trophy.

Being accustomed to seeing fallow deer and red deer in Germany, she was impressed with this bull.

Katerina and Bill with her late season bull.

My long time friend and frequent hunting guest, Bruce Moe came up in September, 1984, and brought along a lady he was seeing.

Carmen was enchanted to be high in the Arctic wilderness and keen to collect as many memories as she could. Soon she expressed her desire to harvest a caribou to place on her wall in Seattle.

There was time enough to acquaint her with my spare rifle, a .300 Winchester magnum. After showing some initial trepidation, she discovered that with proper handling, the recoil was tolerable.

We had large bands of caribou coming down the valley on a daily basis. One overcast afternoon we found a "taker" bull on the northwest alluvial fan. The stalk was simple and direct and with one shot, Carmen became a big game hunter.

I believe this lady would have been totally satisfied if she had not taken a trophy, but collecting this good bull topped off her first Arctic experience.

Carmen and her first big game trophy.

A local girl.

In July, 1984, at the Miss Kotzebue beauty judging contest I met a local woman who had married and moved to the "south forty-eight." Kathy had returned to her home town to visit relatives and think about her life. She was going through a divorce which had been a long time in the making.

She knew that I was a guide and made a point of telling me that her husband had never taken her hunting, though she had longed for such an adventure for many years.

We became friends and the following September, after her divorce was finalized, I took her in the floatplane to look over some of the wild country to which she had never been exposed. We had practiced shooting with a .270, shooting targets on the beach south of town.

About mid-afternoon of our sightseeing flight we came upon some mature bull caribou, one of which had all the components of a really good rack. It showed six or seven points on the top beams, exceptional bez and a well developed single shovel. This would be a dandy animal for her first harvest.

But the band of caribou was traveling through open tundra, offering no way to stalk to within shooting distance. I wanted her to get a reasonably close shot under calm conditions. It would be terrible for her to make a sloppy kill on her first animal.

The caribou were trekking in a well worn trail which wove between open tundra lakes.

Taking caribou on the same day one was airborne was legal and commonly done in those days.

I landed the cub about a mile ahead of the small herd that held the one I wanted for her. After securing the aircraft we walked to the edge of the lake and waited patiently for less than thirty minutes, as the mob of tundra deer came to us. We were directly downwind of the caribou, which is the only species of big game that I know of that typically walks downwind. These animals remained true to their nature and kept coming. The desired bull was near the back of a herd of about forty animals bound for our lake. With most of the herd already past our position, the right bull came by within fifty yards of our prone position.

What a nice start to a hunting life.

It took little coaching for the lady to squeeze off a shot. The bull dropped straight down on all fours and remained in that position. It was stone dead. The lady seemed surprised.

My sister, Pat, and I hunted big game together since we were in grade school, beginning with Collared Peccaries in Arizona. In 1984 Pat passed her Registered Guide examination and helped me with hunters at Trail Creek for several years.

Pat with guest Jim White and a dandy grizzly taken a mile from the lodge.

The cook takes a bull before brunch.

In 2016 my daughter, Bess, the elder of our second batch of kids, came to cook at the lodge. Her mother had taught her well and the meals were complimented by everyone.

Ron and I had our hands full taking care of our four guest hunters, but late one afternoon, an opportunity came for Bess to step away from the stove and harvest her first caribou. It was a young, lone cow. Bess shot well and helped with the butchering before returning to begin the evening meal for seven people.

My wife, Mae enjoyed hunting.

My wife Mae loved to hunt and accompanied me on many pursuits. When we were market hunting, we would usually shoot a minimum of ten caribou per day. The Cessna 180 on hydraulic wheel skis could transport ten gutted and beheaded carcasses from the bush to town where the going rate for a properly shot animal (meaning head shot) was thirty-five dollars. We did the market hunting only for a

Bess and me with her caribou taken on the lodge runway.

The Cessna 180 could haul ten carcasses plus pilot and passenger.

few years, in late spring, as the vast herds migrated north.

Mae's passing in 1983 was a crippling event for me. She was the finest hunting partner I ever had.

Mae was probably the only Alaskan Inuit woman ever to harvest a large male leopard in Southern Rhodesia.

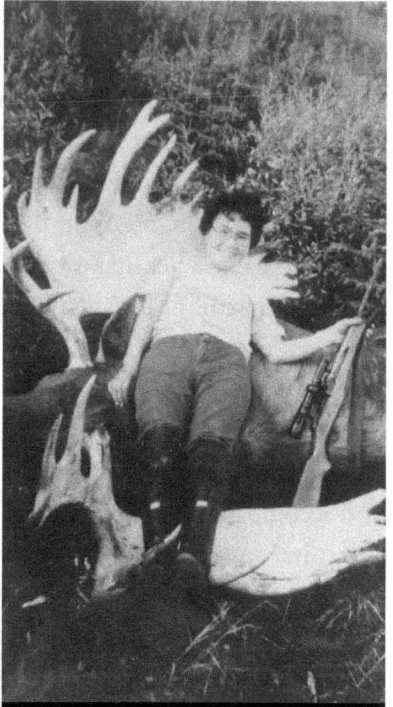

We took a bull moose every year for our own freezer. This was 1978.

Mae and our daughter Sandy with Sandy's ram.

Chapter Eighteen

The Guy Who Never Got His Deer

Back in the early 1980s I had a Single Side Band High Frequency radio transceiver at the lodge and another at our home in Kotzebue. This provided wonderfully dependable communications - most of the time.

We used a simple dipole antenna for each set, which was merely two copper antenna wires of equal length radiating laterally from the radio in approximately opposite directions.

In most weather conditions we could communicate reliably with Kotzebue, which is 118 miles south of the lodge. Occasionally I had some unexpected, but interesting conversations with boats in the Bering Sea and the Gulf of Alaska.

Suddenly our transmissions were usually not so good, and I did not believe it was caused by adverse atmospheric conditions. I mentioned this to a local fellow, Mike, who worked for the Federal Aviation Administration. He looked at the set at our home, tested a couple of tubes, and deemed it to be in fine working order, then suggested that I bring the other set from the lodge for him to check.

During our conversation over a glass of wine at my home, Mike mentioned that he had been hunting many times, but was never successful in getting even a shot at a deer, let alone bagging one.

Aha! I asked him if he would like to check the radio at my camp and perhaps spend an overnight. If caribou were in the area, he might bag one on the same trip. I was planning a freight trip to the lodge and had room for a passenger.

My bookings that fall had a blank spot between guests during which I planned to fly up a load of supplies, so Mike could go on that trip which was scheduled for the next day. He arranged to be absent from work and up we went with my labrador, Zeke, riding on his lap.

This young man had not been in the back country and eagerly agreed to go whenever such an opportunity arose. He said that even in the event that we saw no caribou, he looked forward to the opportunity to see some wild country.

I had long since become accustomed to having "Murphy," author of "Murphy's Law," riding on my shoulder, but this time old Murphy must have been taking a nap.

Wanting to entertain the young fellow, I flew a more scenic route at low level, rather than the direct route at higher elevation. We crossed from the headwaters of the Kugororuk River into the Trail Creek drainage and were thrilled to see several bands of hundreds of caribou headed directly toward the lodge.

My passenger was breathless, as well as speechless. When he got his thoughts collected he said he had never seen so many "deer" in his entire life. Mike's excitement was contagious and was immediately contracted by my dog, Zeke, who poked the back of my seat with his nose to make sure I saw the game as well.

In those days there was no closed season and no limit on caribou in northwest Alaska, nor was there any restrictions on shooting caribou the same day airborne. Caribou meat could be legally sold and several residents of Kotzebue provided fresh meat at thirty-five dollars per carcass.

We landed ten minutes later, but saw no animals near the lodge. However the ones we had just flown over were following trails used by most of the southward bound animals that season. I was confident that we would see plenty of caribou later that evening or the next morning. And weather was forecast to be good for the next two days.

As we packed the supplies to the lodge my guest kept stopping to lay down his load and bring up his binoculars as he nervously scanned the area in hopes of spotting caribou.

In short time Mike had checked out my transceiver, found a touch of corrosion on one connection, cleaned it, showed me how to better maintain the radio, and on schedule that evening, the radio worked fine.

But we saw no caribou until too late to make a stalk. A few dozen animals had moved in on the alluvial fan across the river from the lodge. I

Two large bands of southward migrating Barren Ground Caribou.

figured them to be the vanguard of the large groups we had flown over and I expected to see many more caribou nearby the next morning.

Mike was sure that with his luck, the animals would be long gone by daylight. I've seen that emotion in others, honed by years of lack of success.

But daylight came and we were surrounded by several hundred caribou. Most were feeding, many were laying down. None seemed in a hurry. It was a scene of natural tranquility.

So we had coffee and a light breakfast before beginning our short stalk.

Glassing from the living room, we saw more mature bulls across the river, so we headed that way. Zeke was even more excited than my guest, who was in a high state of twitch.

We climbed the tall cutback and peered across the wide alluvial fan. We had not noticed a young animal close by that jumped up on its hind legs and ran toward the large group with nose and tail in the air.

"Oh no," whispered my companion, but the yearling caribou stopped and turned to look back at us. We froze in place. The wind was light and coming from up the valley. The animal had not gotten our scent. When the youngster began to slowly walk toward the big group, occasionally stopping to graze, we retreated down the cut bank and climbed it again about two hundred yards further downstream, and downwind.

We stopped in a small gully with decent willow brush for cover and waited until several mature bulls were less than one hundred yards from us. The caribou were walking downwind, as they commonly do.

Mike was getting anxious, so I whispered to pick the bull with antlers he liked best and shoot it. I handed him my walking stick with a fork at the top to use as a gun rest. Zeke knew what was coming and his otter-tail was smacking my leg with metronomic regularity.

I watched as Mike aimed - his rifle muzzle was not steady, so I put my hand on his shoulder and whispered to take his time as there was no reason to rush.

The report of his rifle was followed by the unmistakable "thump" of lead hitting meat. The caribou spun around and staggered. Before I could tell Mike to hold, he shot again and another bull fell. Thereupon the first bull collapsed.

The guest who "never got his deer," with his two headed caribou.

Mike told me he thought he was aiming at the first caribou. The two bulls were standing next to each other and were very similar in antler confirmation and size. This was not the first time such a thing had happened, nor would it be the last, and it was good as I had room enough to take the meat of two animals to town.

After spilling the guts, I counted two ribs up from the most posterior rib, cut through and halved each carcass. We tied a hind half on each of our pack boards and took the fat, prime meat to the aircraft.

We came to the crest of the big cut bank and saw two grey wolves on the stream just below. The wolves appeared to see us at the same instant. They turned and disappeared into the thick willows in a flash. For Mike that was more unique stimulation on top of what we had already enjoyed. Sight of the two lobos lightened our loads and added spring to our steps. What a day!

The second trip we tied on the front halves. It always surprises newcomers to learn that the front is heavier than the hind half. We had the meat back to the airplane in two loads each. It took only about one hour of packing.

We enjoyed a quick lunch and a ninety minute flight to town. All in all, it had been a great short trip. Mike's years-long run of unproductive hunting was at its end.

Chapter Nineteen
Clumsy Kills

Pistol shot bull.

It was a bit past mid-September of 1979. I had flown a load of aviation gasoline and stove oil up to the cabin on Trail Creek. The wind was light and the temperature warm for that time of year and latitude.

I had no compelling reason to not sit back and enjoy the moment. It had been a hectic summer, as usual. I got in over two hundred hours of charter flying, mostly in Shellabarger's Cessna 180 on floats. I had some small building projects well under way in Kotzebue. Our guest hunters had taken their animals and departed. We were blessed with a surprise stretch of pleasant "Indian summer" conditions, but the conditions were forecast to turn sour after only a few days of climatic glory.

Gasoline and stove oil were kept outside in round five-gallon cans which, unlike the older square sided cans, bears seemed unable to puncture.

I used the ladder to get on the first story roof, then put my platform astraddle the second story ridge line and took up a folding chair from which to sit and glass the valley, and maybe doze a little before flying the one and a half hours to town. My labrador, Zeke, did not like being left on the ground and he occasionally whimpered, so I brought him up on the lower roof. After a few minutes I observed a mature bull caribou coming down the valley along the route that had been used by most of the animals that year. He was headed for the swampy bog adjacent to the willows that surrounded the cabin.

We didn't need any more meat, but an elderly neighbor lady could use some, so, I thought why not harvest this prime critter for her? I would feel bad to not do this for Mamie Beaver. I always enjoyed her company and stories. I could cut the carcass in half and pack it to the runway in two loads in just thirty minutes, or less.

Old square side gas cans on left, round cans stacked on the right.

But I'd not figured on doing any hunting and had left my rifle in town. If I was to take that animal, my .44 magnum pistol would have to do. If the bull continued on the same course I could intercept him from the willows and maybe have a shot at thirty yards or less. I checked the cylinder and found it held six rounds. I should only need one shot to deck that animal.

This was not a trophy animal, but it's bez would make fine backscratchers and a dog sled maker in town could use the rest of the antlers in his craft. I would feel criminally negligent to not take advantage of this opportunity.

So, leaving the chair on the roof, Zeke and I quietly made our way to the willows closest to which the bull would be walking. The animal, a straggler of the large herds that had previously passed, kept plodding toward us, head down and seemingly oblivious to his surroundings. I wondered if he was sleep walking. He looked fat and prime.

When he came to the point nearest us, using a walking stick to steady my hand, I carefully drew a bead on the base of his neck and fired. The noise rudely interrupted the silent tranquility of the valley. As the bull reared up, I noticed his right foreleg hanging limp. My shot had struck him low and left of my intended point of impact. The animal looked directly

Clumsy Kills

at me and turned to quickly stumble-run across the swampy bog and up a low knoll. There he stopped and looked back at me from about eighty yards away. I felt bad. Again using my walking stick to steady my aim I fired, but the lead struck tundra instead of meat.

Now Zeke was excited. He whined, asking for permission to intercede in my behalf, but I told him to stay.

Now the range had become close to one hundred yards. I needed a closer shot.

Caribou are not stupid and this one did his best to put distance between himself and whatever devilish irritant he had encountered - that would be me.

When the wounded bull topped over the knoll and went out of sight, Zeke and I sprinted around the downwind side of the hill and found ourselves within fifty yards of the confused and wounded animal.

I had never lost a wounded big game animal of my own except for one deer years ago - which still bothered me - and I didn't want to lose this caribou. Thinking I may not get as close a shot again, I used the walking stick to steady my aim and squeezed the trigger. The only result was the rude report of the firearm's discharge. It was another miss. The moss and lichen covered tundra gave no hint of where the bullet impacted.

This time the stricken bull charged straight up hill, but soon turned right to quarter along the slope. I had only three shots left and no replacement ammunition in my pocket. Zeke may have been counting my shots too as he was pleading with me to let him "take" our quarry. I had never allowed a dog to chase big game and I kept telling Zeke to stay. Difficult as it was for him, he obeyed.

By this time a body shot just aft of the withers was my goal. I missed another shot, then another. One shot left. Rats, I never was proficient with a pistol.

But the bull was stressed to the maximum and stumbled as he continued up the slope. After a half hour, he stopped and stood broadside to me at about sixty yards. I careful fired again and the bull went down. This round had broken a hind leg below the knee. This is not the way I recommend taking a big game animal, but now, at least, I could reach the poor beast.

As the caribou struggled to gain its footing, Zeke just couldn't hold it any longer. My fine dog broke for the bull and maneuvered himself to the

My expression shows a mix of relief and disgust at my performance.

uphill side of the of the stricken caribou, then he jumped and had the bull on the ground. I was afraid one of the antler tines would impale my dog, so as the bull focused on Zeke, I was able to get a hand on each antler and twist the animal to expose its throat. I want the reader to know that stressed and wounded adult caribou bull was powerful beyond my expectation. The sheer terror in his eyes bothered me, and haunts me still.

I plunged my knife into the throat of the caribou and slashed outward to draw a fountain of jugular blood. I stepped back, called Zeke to my side, and watched the big bull bleed out. I never want to kill another animal that way! I was relieved that the animal did not escape to die on its own after an indeterminate amount of suffering, but in making such a prolonged, sloppy kill - I felt derelict in my duty as a hunter - and a human.

Coming in we had flown over a sow grizzly with two cubs that were easily within range to hear my shooting and locate us. Zeke and I hurried back to the cabin to get more rounds for the pistol, in case the bears visited us. As I put on my pack board, and I grabbed a tripod and camera for a photograph.

The remainder of the afternoon was routine. I cut the animal in two pieces, and made two trips to the runway. Time was flying. I had spent over two hours in this endeavor, so I quickly pulled the chair and platform off the roof, closed up the cabin and headed home.

Mamie was pleased to receive the meat from that fat bull, Albert appreciated the antlers, and I sawed off the bez for two backscratchers.

Regrettable Harvest

Part of the allure of hunting is the fact that we do not control the events or outcome of our pursuits. We, after all, are not shooting fish in a barrel or smashing cockroaches in the kitchen sink.

Over the past sixty-five years I have introduced more than a couple dozen youngsters to the world of hunting. With each young person, boy or girl, we discussed and practiced gun safety, marksmanship, stewardship of wild game, and basic ethics, prior to going to the field. We studied the life cycles and habits of the game we sought. We discussed the letting of blood and its necessity in most hunting endeavors. I emphasized the clean and proper care of meat. I wanted my charges to be as prepared as possible for extended periods of inactivity, brief moments of high excitement, and, most of all, profound respect for the game they pursued. I wanted no one to be shocked by the sight of blood or the brief reaction or struggle of their prey after the impact of the bullet. I hoped and expected none to be revulsed by the sight of blood. I emphasized that with a carefully placed shot, the animal should drop cleanly and hopefully not thrash about, but sometimes, even a perfect shot may result in the animal convulsing or kicking. Clean kills are the goal.

Finally, we discussed the possibility of wounding an animal and not recovering it. The thought of leaving a crippled animal to die, possibly after a lingering, prolonged agony is abhorrent. On rare occasions it may prove to be unavoidable, but we must do all that is humanly possible to avoid leaving a wounded animal in the field.

Cottontail rabbits or hares were usually the first animals we pursued for the table. On two occasions I spent more than two hours with a protege looking for, and eventually finding a wounded bunny. In each case we celebrated our hard-won success. On the first such occasion in Arizona we noticed a speck of blood at the cholla cactus strewn entrance to a pack rat's burrow. Luckily one of the cottontail's rear feet was visible just past the entrance of the burrow. The animal had died right there. We were able to tease it out with a stick.

In 1970 I took my daughter Sandy caribou hunting. We were using a wall tent at our homestead site before we built the first little cabin. Some guests from Montana had taken caribou and Sandy expressed interest in hunting one. We had a lever action 30/30 in camp which her mother used. We kept it in the tent in case of need of bear protection or desire to harvest a caribou. Lever action "John Wayne" carbines are great for all beginners as everyone has seen their use in western movies, and with the simple outside hammer, the safety is truly safe.

So we had a few days to spend just with the immediate family. This should provide the opportunity for which Sandy yearned.

The next day we watched dozens of caribou come down from the north. The migrating beasts were traveling at a rapid clip, so Sandy and I hustled to intercept a small band. Our dog, Zeke was with us. The wind was in our favor, but something spooked the cow in the lead and she turned her band up into the narrow, rocky canyon we call Break Ankle. Sandy and I slowly proceeded along the side of the canyon opposite to that of the caribou. We weren't gaining on the moving group of caribou so I had Sandy single out the animal she wanted, get comfortably positioned using my pack board on the ground for a rest, take careful aim and shoot the bull. The distance across the canyon was around one hundred and twenty yards.

She fired and the bull went down. Sandy shrieked in joy, but the caribou got to its feet and began to struggle after the rest of its group. Sandy shot again and the bull fell again. She had broken both legs low on the animal's left side. The pitiful animal struggled to regain its footing, only to repeatedly fall and roll a short way down the hill. The caribou was obviously terrified. I was feeling really bad. This was Sandy's first big game animal kill and I hoped its horrible development would not sour her on hunting.

By the time we reached the still struggling animal it had stopped in a shallow swale near the bottom of the canyon. I told Sandy she should shoot it in the neck, as close to the back of the head as possible. She did just that.

I was embarrassed and agonizing over how the innocent wild beast had been subjected to such a horrific end of its life. I felt responsible. I feared Sandy would never want to shoot another animal.

As we sat next to the dead bull I asked Sandy if she would ever like to shoot another one. She brought her head up immediately, looked around, and asked "Where?"

A Long Range Knock-down

I've never been in favor of long range shots, except in cases where an already wounded animal was about to escape or enter an area from which retrieval would be compromised. I figure the closer the shot the better, but anything up to three hundred yards should be acceptable for an experienced rifleman. I tell guests to come prepared to shoot up to that distance.

To my way of thinking the real essence and satisfaction of hunting lies in the stalk. Ideally, this endeavor culminates with arriving at reasonable shooting distance from the quarry. In some cases, particularly with wary, open country game such as sheep and caribou, a stalk to within close enough range, or even reasonable range, may not be in the cards. In such cases, I usually end the pursuit without shooting in hopes of resuming it when the animal calms down, or perhaps on the following day.

For everyone, stretching the range, by shooting much over three hundred yards, multiplies the chances for a bad shot and crippling the animal without immobilizing it. The field variables including wind at different directions and velocities between the shooter and the target, less than ideal stability for the shooter who may be standing on a slope or uneven ground, the shooter being winded or fatigued, the shooter's overall experience, and other factors individually or collectively may contribute to the bullet striking the animal at other than the preferred spot. The gut cavity makes up approximately half of the center of mass of the broadside silhouette of a big game animal, and in fact the gut seems to draw projectiles fired from excessively long ranges more than its size would indicate. I feel it is unfair to the animal to attempt to shoot at excessive range.

A few years ago we had two guests from Nevada and two from Florida at the lodge. I took the Nevada boys north, but returned empty handed by mid-afternoon. My assistant, Ron, and the Floridians had gone south. As I looked out the window, cup of coffee in hand, I saw the young fellow from Florida coming down the hillside from the East Bowl. He was moving as rapidly as he could. I wondered what was up.

He said that they had found three caribou bulls, but none met his or his Dad's expectations (both had taken statewide Big Three award winning top three caribou with us in previous years, so they knew what they were seeing), but, they reasoned, maybe the Nevada men would like to shoot one. That was thoughtful. But this was the first hunting day of their booking and the Nevada fellows said they had walked enough.

I told the enthusiastic young man that if he wanted to shoot the largest of the bulls, he could do so without having to pay a trophy fee. Multiple caribou were legal for non-residents. He would only have to buy the non-resident tag which cost $325 in those days.

Each hunter already carried one caribou tag and I could sell more if needed at the lodge. The young man hustled off. He seemed to almost fly up the hill to rejoin his Dad and Ron.

I did some puttering around with firewood for the sauna as I got dinner laid out and glassed for game. After a bit more than an hour I saw the three fellows coming off the eastern hills. By their body language I figured they were not pleased.

Story was, by the time the young hunter joined Ron and his Dad, the caribou were well over 600 yards away. Ron began the stalk, but the animals were aware of the hunters and began moving higher and further from our guests. The Floridians were sure they could take the biggest bull at a that range. Ron counseled against shooting. If not disturbed, the animals might be hanging around the next day, but the Florida boys began to shoot. After several shots the biggest bull went down hard, as if pole-axed!

There was some pretty wild whooping and high-fives briefly before Ron told them the bull was back on his feet.

Then a true barrage began, but the caribou walked on, seemingly undisturbed. The shooters ran out of ammunition.

When the shooters recounted the events to me I told them that I believed the bull had been struck either in the spinous processes of the neck or in an antler. Either such case usually results in a dramatic knock-down, followed by a quick return to the upright position and departure from the area. Neither of such a bullet strike is fatal or even debilitating, but the animal must be followed to ascertain that it is not seriously wounded.

Clumsy Kills

The shovel had a 7mm hole in it.

The following morning I took the two Florida hunters back up the eastern hills in pursuit of the caribou. After nearly three hours we found a grazing bull that met the description of the one that had been hit. This time we stalked to within one hundred yards. The young man took a solid rest and knocked it to the ground with a shot to the neck.

It is amazing that being hit in the antler could have such an immediate, dramatic effect on a large animal, but it happens. I have seen this take place on four other occasions with caribou, once with moose and twice with deer.

All Caribou are atypical…. but…

I can't send a book on Caribou off to the publisher without mentioning this unusual situation I encountered with three Argentinians. I wrote of this experience in my book, Alaska Tales, Laughs and Surprises, so I will be brief here.

Like Germans, Argentinians seem to hold non-typical trophies in high esteem. Caribou antlers show more variations than do the head bones of most deer, but true atypism is rare and hard to evaluate in *Rangifer tarandus*.

One morning we glassed an unusual sight. One small bull in a band of caribou was carrying what appeared to be a large, grossly malformed and abnormal set of antlers.

The guests pronounced it "Abnorme, abnorme."

As the animals came closer I was convinced we were seeing willow roots entangled with the beast's natural headgear, but my guests would hear nothing of that. The shooting began.

Only when they approached the dead bull did they believe it was not a world record class nontypical caribou.

I suggested we might retain the roots on the trophy, but the hunter declined.

Unusual, but not atypical or abnormal for Caribou.

Chapter Twenty
Spend an Extra Day

The spring and summer of 2018 were discouraging with several guest hunter cancellations - all for valid reasons. In a low volume operation like I have always run, any cancellation is bad, but multiple cancellations are devastating financially. This fall we were left with only two guest hunters. In addition to that, ole Murphy was with us and hyper-active the entire time.

So Ron and I had only one hunter each to help secure trophies. One fellow, Dick, had hunted with me on two previous occasions, our other guest had read my books and decided to hunt with us based on my stories.

Both men were truly gentleman.

From the lodge windows we glassed a blond grizzly on the second day of the booking. On his previous hunts, Dick had taken two caribou and one grizzly. He generously suggested that the other guest, Art, have first option on the blond bear.

This bear was moving from one berry patch to the next, not unlike a kid in a candy shop. After a few munches it would sometimes rare up on its hind legs and run a few steps before lowering its head and slurping up more berries. This animal was obviously having a deliciously wonderful time partaking of the natural summer bounty offered by the foothills.

Ron got Art within a couple hundred yards of the frolicking bruin, but it was early in a twelve day hunt, he suggested Art hold off on shooting. There should be plenty more opportunities before the day of departure came.

In the next two days we observed a small band of caribou drifting lazily down the valley, but as usual for the early caribou movements, most were cows with calves accompanied by only young bulls. We concentrated on enjoying the abundant berries, as the grizzly was doing.

Two days later Ron and Art found a large, dark brown grizzly digging roots in the stream bed, but as they approached, a rogue zephyr carried their smell to the bear and it charged off into thick brush offering no opportunity for a shot.

But on day six, we spotted a group of eight mature bulls traveling down the valley across from the lodge. One was truly outstanding, but the rest were not impressive. Dick generously offered Art the option of going after the big one.

Art and Ron were booted up and headed across the valley to intercept the walking bulls in minutes. When caribou appear to be walking casually, in fact they are usually traveling much faster than a man can walk, so haste is usually in order.

The men timed it right and waited in a copse of willows in a depression just in front of the band of caribou. A light breeze drifted from the animals to the hunters. Art shot the impressive bull at about forty yards.

Everyone was elated. I predicted that this rack would score high enough to place in the top three in the annual Big Three competition. In fact, it placed number two.

This bull is a taker any day.

Dick enjoyed some stream fishing and caught some small Arctic Char in our dip water creek near the sauna.

Caribou traffic increased over the next week with an occasional trophy bull in amongst the cows and calves, but Dick and I were flummoxed each time we attempted a stalk. On one occasion we were wadded up in a small gut of the cutback off the end of the runway with caribou walking within twenty yards of our position, but the impressive bulls were bunched with lesser animals, offering no unobstructed shot. Similar disappointments plagued us on three other occasions.

Art collected the blond grizzly on his last day of the booking, which I detailed in the story "The Eleventh Hour Grizzly."

As we had no more guest hunters coming in, I urged Dick to stay on for another day or so, but due to his schedule, he declined the offer.

Our two guests left around noon. Two hours later, I shot two large bulls for meat near the runway. Either animal would have delighted Dick or most any other hunter. So it goes, sometimes.

Not an outstanding rack, but worth another day of hunting.

www.ingramcontent.com/pod-product-compliance
Lightning Source LLC
Chambersburg PA
CBHW071710160426
43195CB00012B/1641